JOHNNY GURKHA

E. D. (Birdie) Smith was born in Scotland and educated in Devon. He joined up in 1942 and saw service with the Brigade of Gurkhas in Italy and Greece. After the war he held various appointments in his Regiment (The Seventh Gurkha Rifles) during the Malayan Emergency and the Confrontation in Borneo. A helicopter crash during the campaign in Sarawak threatened to end his life and career as a soldier, but, although he lost his right arm, he survived to command the 1/2nd King Edward VII's Own Gurkha Rifles in Borneo, Brunei and Hong Kong.

After leaving the Army in 1978, Birdie Smith was a bursar and part-time teacher before deciding to concentrate on his writing.

JOHNNY GURKHA

'Friends in the Hills'

E. D. Smith

ARROW BOOKS

Arrow Books Limited
62-65 Chandos Place, London WC2N 4NW

An imprint of Century Hutchinson Limited

London   Melbourne   Sydney   Auckland
Johannesburg and agencies throughout
the world

First published by Leo Cooper in association with
Martin Secker & Warburg Ltd 1985
Arrow edition 1987

Printed and bound in Great Britain by
Anchor Brendon Limited, Tiptree, Essex

ISBN 0 09 951080 4

To my friends in the hills

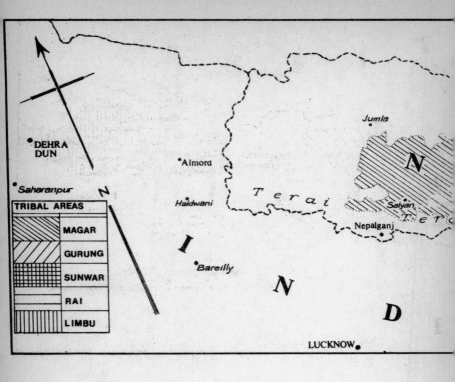

CONTENTS

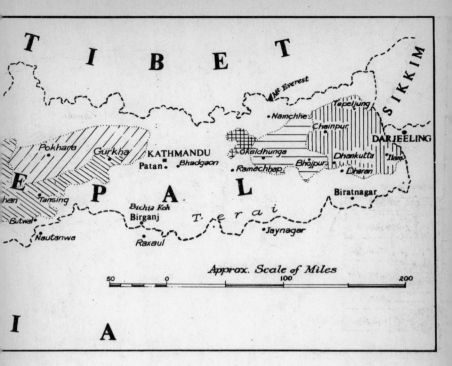

ACKNOWLEDGEMENTS

For the ready help they have afforded me, my thanks are due to Brigadier Chris Pike, DSO, OBE, and his staff at HQ Brigade of Gurkhas; the Secretaries of all ten Gurkha Regimental Associations; and, in particular, to Lt-Col H. C. S. Gregory, OBE (late 10 GR) for reading the manuscript as well as making constructive suggestions.

All the following, shown in alphabetical order, contributed with stories, previous articles, or suggestions: Hon Lt Aitasing Gurung, MC; Lt-Col M. G. Allen; Major J. A. Anderson; Rfn Baliprasad Rai; Sgt Basant Kumar Dewan; Sgt Bishan Dewan; Lt-Col T. G. Blackford; Capt J. Burton-Page; Col J. P. Cross, OBE; Hon Capt Dalbahadur Limbu, IOM, MC; Col R. A. N. Davidson, OBE; Lt-Col J. A. I. Fillingham, OBE; Major C. N. Fraser; Capt (QGO) Dipakbahadur Gurung MVO; Lt-Col H. R. K. Gibbs; Capt C. J. Gowland; Col E. R. Hill, OBE; Sgt Jasbahadur Gurung, Lt-Col C. E . Jarvis; Major D. Llewellyn-Davies; Lt-Col A. A . Mains; Major Maniprasad Rai; Major C. M. McCausland; Lt-Col W. D. McNaughton, MBE; Lt-Col D. P. Morgan, OBE; Col E. D. Murray, DSO, OBE; Major C. N. J. Nicholas; Col P. H. D. Panton, CBE; Lt-Col E. M. H. Parsons, DSO; Major J. M. Patrick; Major J. Rennie; Major D. L. Purves, MBE, TD; Major-General J. A. R. Robertson, CB, CBE, DSO; Major M. C. A. R. Roberts, MC; Lt-Col C. J. Scott, OBE; Major F. Turner; General Sir Walter Walker, KCB, CBE, DSO; J. J. Waters; Major P. H. J. Wilcocks; Major M. R. Willis; W. Winchester; Lt-Col C. G. Wylie.

To them all, my gratitude and to anyone who has been omitted from the list, my apologies. I am also grateful for the assistance given me by the written works of Lieutenant-General Sir Francis Tuker, John Masters and Professor Sir Ralph Turner—all of them, alas, no longer with us. Living writers whose works have inspired me with ideas include J. M. Marks, Dennis Sheil-Small, Harold James and Peter Pitt; with the permission of the publishers, some quotations appears from my own books and articles.

To Miss Frances Shepherd my profound gratitude for typing and re-typing drafts as well as deciphering my intricate corrections which must have tried her patience more than somewhat on numerous occasions.

The photographs are reproduced with the kind permission of the Editor of *The Kukri*, Major Robin Adshead (late 6th Queen Elizabeth's Own Gurkha Rifles) and the Commandant 1st Battalion 7th Duke of Edinburgh's Own Gurkha Rifles.

The map of Nepal was drawn by Captain R. C. Read, former Assistant Hydrographer of the Royal Navy.

PREFACE

Johnny Gurkha: a story of Loyalty and Comradeship

> 'Well done, Gurkhas, keep moving Gurkhas' still rings in my ears.
> At times so deeply moved, we felt like crying with joy and pride
> for we found in the middle of the London streets how close and
> dear we are to the British people.

With the cheers of the crowds still resounding in the background,
those words were written by Sergeant Basantkumar Dewan after he
had taken part in the 1982 London Marathon as a member of the 7th
Gurkha Rifles' team.

Why have the British people, many of whom know next to nothing
about the Gurkhas, taken them to their hearts? It is an intriguing
question and one which prompted me to write this book, supported
by contributions from many people.

Inevitably, there are comparatively few anecdotes recorded from
the nineteenth century so that the earlier pages concentrate on
the historical background; without some fabric and chronological
sequence, the stories would have lost much of their impact. To those
readers who do not want too much history, be of good cheer; the
doses later in the book are small and injected at irregular intervals!

As will be seen from the acknowledgements, many people have
helped me to to produce this tribute; I am grateful to them for their
unstinting help and co-operation and hope they will understand why
most of their efforts are shrouded in anonymity. For the general
reader the text would not have been improved by a continuous flow
of names of people, known only to the Brigade. So, Lt-Col Snooks
becomes 'a retired officer'—and so on. This is an important point
because this book has been written for the general reader, although I

hope that the 'old and bold', as well as the serving members of today's Brigade, will find enjoyment in its pages. Certainly it has been a labour of love, especially when friends and acquaintances from the past have taken the trouble to contact me and, by so doing, have brought back memories of experiences shared while serving with our friends, the Gurkhas.

DHANYABAD (thank you)

GLOSSARY

Ama	Mother
Ayo Gurkha	'The Gurkha comes' (war-cry!)
Baba or *Ba*	Father
Bahun	Brahmin priest
CT	Communist Terrorist (Malayan Emergency)
ECO	Emergency Commissioned Officer
Guru-ji	Honoured/respected teacher
Havildar	Sergeant
INA	Indian National Army (renegades in the Second World War)
Keta	Lad, boy
KGO	King's Gurkha Officer (during George VI's reign, 1948 until his death)
Khajana	Treasure (used for 'ammunition' in years gone by)
Khola	River
Khud-race	Race up and down (steep) hillside
Line boys	Male offspring, born in the regiment
Madal	Two-ended oval-shaped drum, one end smaller to give higher note, beaten with the hands at either end
Maruni	A male dancer dressed in feminine costume, playing a woman's part in religious or folk dance
MRLA	Malayan Races Liberation Army (during Communist-led Emergency)

Naik	Corporal
Nepali	Lingua franca of Nepal, derived from Sanskrit. Usually recorded in Deva Nagri characters, although it can be written in Roman script.
OTS	Officer Training School (in India during the Second World War)
Paltan	Battalion, unit
Porsenge	Male dancer in traditional costume
QGO	Queen's Gurkha Officer (during Queen Elizabeth II's reign)
Raksi	Rum; spirits
Sangar	A stone breastwork
Shabash (or more accurately, *Shyabash*)	Well done!
Shikar	Prey; game; hunting
Subedar	Senior Viceroy Commissioned Officer, usually second-in-command of a company
Suttee	Now abolished Hindu custom of widow sacrificing herself on dead husband's funeral pyre

PROLOGUE

'Friends in the Hills'

Way up in the foothills of the Himalayas, a young Gurkha shepherd boy was grazing a flock of goats on the high pastures above the roaring River Mewa. The year was probably 1948 but it could well have been a century before because the deep gorge of the Mewa Khola, with the snowy peak of the Topke pushing up into the clouds, had not changed, nor had the sparsely populated countryside below with but a few farmhouses dotted around. In one such farmhouse lived Padambahadur Limbu and his family and it was his youngest son, Manbahadur, who had been entrusted with the goats up in a lonely pasture. It was a solitary life but Manbahadur never found it a boring one. Although the young boy worried about his flock and did his best to stop the goats from straying too far, he also found time to dream about his future life when he hoped to become a soldier.

Like his father and grandfather, as well as various uncles and cousins before him, he hoped to enlist in the army on or after his sixteenth birthday, provided, of course, that he was big enough and lucky enough, because he knew that there would be many trying for the few vacancies. And if he was fortunate he would be accepted. Comparatively uneducated though he was, Manbahadur had innate intelligence and had learnt to stand on his own feet at an early age.

Being a shepherd up in the high pastures, the young boy soon added another skill to that of self-reliance, that of tracking. One day a fine young goat was missing, even after hours of searching by Padambahadur and his sons. When the remains were found a few days later the boy resolved that he would learn to read the language of the ground. There was no one to train him: he learnt by following one of the goats until he was able to notice tiny variations in depth

and outline and differences between one pad print and another. Day
after day he practised his skill so that he was able to recognize the
prints as if they were the signatures of their owners.

In time Manhabadur did join the army, after helping his father to
track a thieving leopard which had begun helping himself to their
goats. The boy's tracking skill astounded his father. Some months
later, in Malaya, young Rifleman Manbahadur earned himself a high
reputation as being the best tracker in D Company of the 7th Gurkha
Rifles. It was his skill which led to the elimination of a much-wanted
Communist terrorist.

Unlike many would-be recruits who vanished from their villages
without warning, Manbahadur Limbu had left home to seek employment as a soldier with his parents' blessings, because, with two other
sons, they knew that there would be no real work for their youngest
on the small farm. Padambahadur had enlisted for a similar reason
and had served with the 7th Gurkha Rifles on the North-West
Frontier. There was nothing unusual in this tradition of sons following fathers' footsteps: men from countless villages had sent their sons
to strange lands thousands of miles away from the Himalayan peaks
overlooking the humble homes of a proud but poor mountain folk.

It is highly improbable that Manbahadur or his friends would have
known that the long friendship between the Gurkhas of Nepal and
the British started not in peace but in war. The seeds of this deep
friendship were sown in a short and bloody war which began in 1814.

ONE

How It All Began

Modern Nepal came into being under the vigorous leadership of Prithwi Narain of Gorkha, founder of the Gorkha nation. After his death in 1792 Nepal entered upon a period of rapid expansion and, as has happened to other nations in modern times, over-reached herself. Using the highly efficient war machine created by Prithwi Narain, the Nepalese rulers conquered Sikkim, including Darjeeling and parts of Tibet in the east, as well as Garhwal and Kumaon in the far west. Further incursions were made into the Dogra country around the fertile Kangra valley.

Conflict with the British, in the shape of the Honourable East India Company, became inevitable. Moreover, by 1814 the British in India had suffered reverses in their encounters with the Mahratta Confederacy. The great moated fortress at Bhurtpore held out against repeated attacks by numerically superior forces under General Lake. In the eyes of the all-victorious Gurkhas, the British appeared to be in a sorry state. The fire-eating Prime Minister of Nepal, Bhim Sen Thapa, was no friend of the British. Addressing his young Rajah in Kathmandu he declared:

> How will the British be able to penetrate into our hills? The small fort of Bhurtpore was the work of man, yet the English, being worsted before it, desisted from the attempt to conquer it. Our hills and fastnesses are formed by the hand of God and are impregnable.

From that time until 1858 every Prime Minister of Nepal was faced with the problem of how to keep a large army employed. Indeed, each year virtually the whole army was disbanded, only to be raised again

a few months later, and this threw a large number of men out of work.
Thus hundreds of trained soldiers were waiting to be recalled to carry
out the only profession they knew, as well as seeking a swift release
from their no-pay condition. To compound this situation all the
upper classes held military rank, even if some of them never went to
war or ever studied their profession.

When the British-Indian Empire reached the Nepalese frontier,
Bhim Sen started a deliberate policy of infiltration through the Terai,
the narrow strip of plain adjoining India. His men absorbed village
after village situated either in areas under dispute or within British
territory itself. These incursions went on for seven years, until open
conflict became inevitable.

Not everybody in Kathmandu was in agreement with Bhim Sen's
forward policy. One of his more famous generals, Amarsing Thapa,
warned the Prime Minister not to stir up the English to the point of
their resorting to arms to settle their differences with Nepal. He
wrote:

> We have hitherto but hunted deer: if we engage in this war, we
> must be prepared to fight tigers ... The advocate of war [Bhim
> Sen] who proposes to fight and conquer the English has been
> brought up in Court and is a stranger to the toil and hardships of
> a military life.

Amarsing voted for peace and advocated the cession to the British of
the disputed villages on the frontier. As the revenue from those
villages was passing into the hands of the Prime Minister's family,
Amarsing's warning went unheeded.

In May, 1814, Gurkha soldiers suddenly raided three frontier
police posts in the Butwal district, killing eighteen policemen and
putting the headman to death with singular brutality. Bhim Sen
received an ultimatum from the Governor-General in India, Lord
Moira, to which his response was: 'If the English want war against
the Gurkha conquerors, they can have it.'

The die had been cast and Lord Moira began assembling his forces
at five centres. He planned to split the invasion army into four
columns: from the Dinapore area General Marley with the main force
of 8,000 men was to march on Kathmandu; from Benares, General
Wood with 4,000 men was to march toward the frontier district of
Butwal and thence into Palpa; from the Saharanpore area, General

Gillespie at the head of 4,000 men was to invade the valley of the Doon, thence to strike towards the capital of Garhwal, Srinagar; finally, General Ochterlony in command of 6,000 men, supported by twelve guns, was to move up the left bank of the River Sutlej and engage Amarsing's main forces at Malaun.

The Company's army, including its allies and detachments, amounted to some 30,000 men with sixty guns. Against this formidable force Bhim Sen had available but 12,000 men. Under Amarsing's nephew, Balbahadur, the nation's crack troops, 600 men of the Purana Gorakh Regiment, were to defend the small fort of Kalunga which stood on a wooded hill, guarding the track to Garhwal, some 500 feet above the surrounding country.

Lord Moira, shortly to be made Marquess of Hastings, had disposed his forces over a 600-mile front and by so doing had extended the defending army. Not only had the Company's armies a vast superiority in numbers but their communications were far more efficient and the four main columns could be supplied and reinforced from the plains behind them. On the other hand Amarsing had lines of communication back to Kathmandu which were truly horrific, involving a two-month walk over narrow winding mountain tracks. The British strategy was to cut that supply route and Gillespie was told to occupy the Doon Valley, thus forcing the Gurkha commander to retreat to the East where he could be attacked and destroyed by Ochterlony and Gillespie. Meanwhile, in the East, the other columns under Marley and Wood were to make for Kathmandu and Palpa, taking full advantage of Gurkha preoccupation in the far West.

This was the first mountain campaign in which the British-Indian army was engaged and the country in which they fought favoured the defenders. Fortunately for Lord Hastings, General David Ochterlony was a born master of operational tactics, a highly efficient commander and bold in spirit. Although lacking any experience of mountain fighting, he devised the stockaded post to protect his main body and was interested to discover, after the first brush with the enemy, that the Gurkhas conducted their defence in a similar manner. Not surprisingly, it was Ochterlony's army that met with success; the other columns forgot to fortify their outposts and met with unwelcome reverses.

For the British-Indian forces new administrative methods had to be adopted. Their heavy artillery and cavalry could no longer be employed; instead of baggage trains of elephants, camels, horses and bullocks, they had to make do with such articles as could be carried on the soldiers' backs and by local porters. No longer could they forage in the invaded country; all their supplies had to be brought up from the plains, often by slow and laborious means. The officers were not able to take hosts of servants with them. An army order decreed that subalterns were allowed three orderlies and captains five, which gives an indication of what campaigning in the plains of India had been like in normal times!

Captain Hearsey, who knew the Nepalese well, wrote of the Gurkha army:

> Their muskets are infamous, and their gunpowder the same. They have little or no clothing and are very ill-paid. They are armed with a musket with or without a bayonet, a sword, and stuck in their girdles is a crooked instrument called a Kookuree. ... They are hardy, endure privations, and are very obedient. ... Under our Government they would make excellent soldiers.

They were an ill-equipped force, although a highly mobile one. Another advantage that the Company had was that the Gurkhas were extremely unpopular in the countries they had recently conquered. As a consequence it did not take very much persuasion or bribery by the British for those who had been subjugated by Nepal to turn on their conquerors.

Formal declaration of war was issued in Lucknow on 1 November, 1814, whereupon the four English columns advanced from their points of forward concentration, only to meet with severe checks all along the line.

The aged General Wood bumped into a stockade near Butwal and his force suffered casualties. Although facing an army half their size, to the disgust of his soldiers, Wood ordered them to withdraw just as the Gurkhas had begun to fall back themselves. Seizing their chance the Gurkhas followed up the British, harassing them unmercifully.

Marley was no more successful, being so dumbfounded by the aggressive spirit shown by the Gurkha hillmen that he ordered his men to move back. Before long, however, he found the responsibility of the operation altogether too much for him; so he quietly rode away by night into self-imposed retirement without telling a soul. He was not the only commander to be sent on pension—on the Nepalese side Bhagatsing had refused to attack Marley's force on the grounds that he was opposed by an army nearly ten times the size of his own. He was ordered back to Kathmandu by Bhim Sen where he faced a court martial and then had to attend an open 'Durbar' dressed in petticoats.

In the West there was a different story to tell. The gallant but ageing Gillespie, still as brave as a lion, seized Dehra Dun, thus further isolating the Gurkha Commander-in-Chief, Amarsing, from his supporting forces. Indeed he was 400 miles from Kathmandu and forced to defend a wide front in recently subjugated and bitterly hostile country. Although the overall British strategy may have had its faults, in the long term it was a sensible one.

In the stockade of Kalunga 600 defenders manned the walls under Balbahadur, watching Gillespie's formidable column of 4,000 men and its guns as it moved towards them. A message offering terms came from the British Commander. Remarking that he did not accept letters so late in the evening, Balbahadur tore it up. On 29 October, 1814, a bombardment was opened with ten guns and the leading troops assembled for the assault, but the initial attacks failed because they were delivered piecemeal and resulted in severe losses.

At the height of the bombardment a Gurkha suddenly appeared, advancing through the shells and smoke, waving his hand. The firing ceased and he was welcomed into the British camp. His lower jaw had been shattered by a shot and he had come for treatment by the British surgeon. When discharged from hospital, he asked for permission to return to his own army in order to fight the British again!

The courageous Gillespie put himself at the head of his old regiment, the Royal Irish Dragoons, to make a third assault on the fort. At his side was Lieutenant Frederick Young, an officer who was to play a large part in the history of the Gurkha Rifles. Dashing towards the gate of the fort, Gillespie was shot down thirty yards from the palisade and died in the arms of Frederick Young.

Again the attack failed, after which the British force waited for over a month until its siege train arrived from Delhi. Once more they assaulted, but with no more success than before. Every time a breach was made the Gurkhas, with their women helping them, drove the assailants back using an assortment of missiles, including bullets, arrows and stones. By this time food and water were running out in the beleagured garrison and Balbahadur was in a desperate plight.

'To capture the fort was a thing forbidden but now I leave of my own accord.' With his last seventy men, the gallant commander slipped away during the night of 1 December and was seen no more

in Kalunga. When the British entered the place there was no one
there save the dead and the grievously wounded, among them women
and children. Balbahadur had lost 520 men, his enemy 31 officers and
750 men. On the hills at Kalunga, now known as Nalapini, are two
small white obelisks, one commemorating Gillespie and those who
fell with him, the other 'their gallant adversary'. 'They fought in fair
conflict like men, and in the intervals of actual combat, showed us a
liberal courtesy,' wrote the British historian.

The one commander who understood how these brave mountain
folk could be defeated was David Ochterlony. ('Old Mahoney' to the
Irish in the 1/87th Regiment.) He was opposed by the experienced
Amarsing Thapa who had 3,000 picked troops under his command.
Amarsing could appreciate good generalship and in his despatches to
Kathmandu he paid tribute to Ochterlony, saying that against him
he could never fight at the time and place of his own choosing. By the
end of October, 1814, Ochterlony was at the foot of the hills where
Amarsing's small force waited. The British had to advance against
the grain of the country, over ridge after ridge, each one well defended
with stockades and fortified posts. Ochterlony conducted a careful
series of operations; step by step he brought his artillery forward to
bear on Amarsing's stronghold at Rangarh. The Gurkha Commander
found that his position was neatly turned so he had no option but to
evacuate it and retreat to Malaun. In spite of the occasional dashing
attack by the Gurkha highlanders, Ochterlony's force pursued a
policy of attrition, probing forward to seize the vantage points they
needed. To make matters worse for Amarsing, the hesitant chiefs of
the district gradually detached themselves from him to join the
British.

The battle for Malaun was won before the actual fighting began;
the wily Ochterlony found that two of the peaks in the very centre of
the Nepalese position were not fortified, a gamble that Amarsing
might have taken against the other British generals but not when
opposed by this one. After a night march, both points fell before
daylight on 15 April and the Gurkha position was neatly bisected. In
fury Amarsing launched all he had, 2,000 men, against the key peak
of Deothal.

'The Gurkhas came on with furious intrepidity, so much so that
several were bayonetted or cut to pieces within our works. Amarsing
stood all the while just within musket range, with the Gurkha

colours planted beside him, while his nephew was everywhere exciting the men to further efforts.'

Gallant, fruitless but disastrous; at the end of the day over 500 Gurkhas lay dead on the field of battle.

Amarsing withdrew his remaining 200 men into the fort of Malaun where he hoped to make a last stand, but realizing that Ochterlony now surrounded his small garrison, he was forced to ask for terms. 'In consideration of the bravery, skill and fidelity with which he had defended the country entrusted to his charge,' Ochterlony agreed that Amarsing should march out with his arms, colours and all his personal property. Courtesy after the battle was one thing but in others the British General was definite and severe. Nepal was to cede to the British the plain of the Terai and to hand back the districts which are today called Kumaon, Garhwal and Simla, to evacuate parts of Sikkim, and, bitterest pill of all, to accept a British Resident at the Court of Kathmandu.

Back in Kathmandu Bhim Sen faltered and evaded. Why should he surrender the Terai, the buffer state that gave Nepal security? Why should they be forced to have a British Resident? Negotiations broke down, especially when Lord Hastings continued to insist that the Terai should pass into British hands. As many of Bhim Sen's nobles drew their income from land they owned in the Terai, the Prime Minister refused the terms. Once again a British force assembled, this time at Dinapore, but again under Sir David Ochterlony, and in January, 1816, 14,000 regular soldiers, supported by irregulars and eighty-three guns, set off to capture Kathmandu. Ochterlony appreciated that the Bichia Koh Pass through the Churiaghati Range would be held in strength and he was determined not to risk a head-on battle for the possession of the defile. To this end he sent officers to reconnoitre tracks to turn its flanks. One of these, Captain Pickersgill, discovered a little-used path through a deep ravine leading up to the heights which overlooked the main position on the pass. Ochterlony did not hesitate and at night led the whole infantry force, with a couple of 5-pounder guns on elephants, in single file through the gorge and by dawn they were shaking out on the high ground.

A further night was spent in acute discomfort as it was bitterly cold. Clothes had been torn to shreds in the ascent and by an oversight rations had not been brought up. The men had not eaten for forty-eight hours and one subaltern recalled that the picquets could be located by the sound of their chattering teeth.

But once again the Gurkhas had been outmanoeuvred and outwitted. Forced to pull back, their small force under Ranjursing withdrew to Makwanpore where, in a final stand, the fighting was intense and bitter. As a British subaltern wrote: 'The havoc was dreadful for they still scorned to fly. On going round the hill afterwards, the dead bodies there astonished me'. At the end of the day there were 500 dead Gurkhas around the British positions; the British losses were about half that number.

It was the beginning of the end. Bhim Sen Thapa was determined that the British would not set foot in the valley of Kathmandu so on 4 March, 1816 he signed a treaty with Sir David Ochterlony. In the latter's words, 'You take either a Resident or War', words which for years were resented in Nepal and made the Resident's task no easier. Fortunately for both countries the early British Residents were men of the highest calibre, Brian Hodgson particularly being outstanding as a statesman and scientist.

During the campaign Ochterlony had recommended the enlistment of Gurkhas in the Company's army, a strange and novel idea at such a time. Shortly afterwards Lieutenant Frederick Young was selected to raise and command an irregular force of 2,000 men for operations on Ochterlony's inner flank. This band of irregulars met the Gurkhas who at once attacked them. The irregulars fled, leaving Young and his handful of officers standing forlorn on what should have been a battlefield. The Gurkhas gathered round and asked why he did not run off with his men.

'I have not come so far in order to run away,' replied Young. 'I came to stop.' And he sat down.

'We could serve under men like you,' observed their leader, a prophetic saying as events were to transpire.

Young was held as an honoured prisoner and treated well, making friends with his captors who taught him their language. When he was released he was sent to look after prisoners-of-war in Dehra Dun where he applied for permission to ask for volunteers to form a Corps of Gurkha soldiers. Permission was granted and as he said afterwards, 'I went there one man and I came out 3,000'. From these men the Sirmoor Battalion was formed, eventually to become the 2nd Gurkhas. This was the small acorn from which was to grow the splendid tree of regular Gurkha battalions which served as part of the

British-Indian Army until 1947, and some of them thereafter as the Brigade of Gurkhas in the modern British Army.

It was to be about these men that Ensign John Shipp of His Majesty's 87th Regiment, himself called the bravest of the brave, was to write in his *Memoirs*:

I never saw more steadiness or bravery exhibited in my life. Run they would not, and of death they seemed to have no fear, though their comrades were falling thick around them, for we were so near that every shot told.

Although the suspicion with which the British Resident was viewed in Kathmandu continued for years to come, in the mountain villages there were scores of men only too willing to go down to India to serve with the 'John Company'.

Strange it is that such a long and lasting friendship should have stemmed from the short but bloody war between 1814 and 1816. That war taught the British to respect the Nepalese highlanders to such an extent that no attempt was ever made to colonize Nepal or coerce that country into becoming part of the Indian Empire. Thus respect and affection was not one-sided. Some years later, when Gurkha soldiers were being praised for their gallantry by British comrades, they returned the flattering partiality of the latter with the following characteristic remark: 'The English are as brave as lions; they are splendid sepoys, and very nearly equal to us!'

TWO

Serving John Company

Smarting over the indignity of defeat, the Nepalese rulers grudgingly consented to some of their troops entering the service of the British Government, if they so wished, and the British Government chose to accept the men. What were they like, these highlanders from Nepal? One observer wrote:

> The genuine Goorkha is recognized by his high cheek-bones, broad Tartar features, small elongated eyes, and the absence of whisker or moustache, with the exception of a few straggling hairs on the upper lip, cherished with great care. As a race, they are considerably below the average height of the natives of Hindustan, broad-chested and bull-necked, with the muscles of the thigh and leg so greatly developed as in some instances to appear unnatural. They are capable of enduring great fatigue, and in their constant sporting excursions amongst the heavy jungles of the Doon or the banks of the Jumna or Ganges with their fishing tackle perform journeys almost incredible to European pedestrians, particularly on their return journey when they generally have a heavy load of venison or fish slung on their shoulders. They are a tractable folk and very amenable to discipline ... Gambling is their besetting vice, and they are thoughtless and improvident in money matters.

While that description might make the modern Gurkha soldier smile in disbelief, the older generation of retired British officers, especially those who served in pre-war India, may nod in agreement. With such qualities it is not surprising that the men who came down out of the hills and offered their services to 'John Company' (the East India

Company) soon won renown as soldiers. The titles of those first local battalions were to change several times over the years that followed but the 1st King George V's Own Gurkha rifles, 2nd King Edward VII's Own Goorkhas and 3rd Queen Alexandra's Own Gurkha Rifles trace their origins back to the original Corps which took service with the East India Company.

In a caste-conscious India it was a great advantage to have soldiers who, in Brian Hodgson's words,

> despatch their meal in half an hour, and satisfy the ceremonial law by merely washing their hands and face and taking off their turbans before cooking, laugh at the pharisaical rigour of the Sipahis [sepoys], who must bathe from head to foot, and make *puja* [worship] ere they can begin to dress their dinners, must eat nearly naked in the coldest weather, and cannot be in marching trim again in less than three hours ... In my humble opinion they are, by far, the best soldiers in India; and if they were made participators of our renown in arms, I can see that their gallant spirit, emphatic contempt of *madhesias* [people living in the plains] and unadulterated military habit, might be relied on for fidelity.

Biased though he undoubtedly was, Brian Hodgson's final remark about fidelity was to be tested and totally upheld during the Indian Mutiny which broke out in 1857. Before that critical year, however, in skirmishes in various parts of India, the mountain warriors began to show their quality and to weave the first strands of the rope that bound the fortunes of Great Britain and Nepal together in mutual esteem during the century and a half that followed.

While the original Gurkha Corps was settling in as part of John Company's army, so did the men seek a permanent location for their families in India. Some idea of the life they led can be gained from the following petition which was delivered to the Commandant at Dehra Dun by the men of the Sirmoor Rifles:

> We, all people of the Battalion, most humbly beg to inform your honour that the old lines of Body Guard is all vacant by several years, also not occupying by anyone, the land is all ruined.

> Therefore we all beg that the same land may be presented to us for making buildings and houses for living of our children and family

persons, because on marching of the Battalion we are taking our children with us, quite trouble takes place . . .

When we were subject to the Rajah of Nepal, all kinds of recommendations were being by him. Now we are children of the Great Hon'ble Company, breeding and educated by them we have no other hope of protection except them.

This quaint petition went to the Government and was the first step in obtaining the permanent regimental home for the 2nd Gurkhas in Dehra Dun. Elsewhere similar arrangements were being made for the other Gurkha units.

In the early Gurkha cantonments could be found many 'line boys'. Most Nepalese recruits had not married before joining their battalions and, with few opportunities to return home, took local women as wives later in their service. The male offspring generally joined the Regiment as 'line boys', becoming bandsmen or clerks, or serving in other administrative posts, because it was considered that their physique and spirit did not measure up to the standard of the true hill Gurkha. There were to be notable exceptions, as we will learn, especially during the Indian Mutiny.

During the first forty years of service under the British, the Gurkhas gradually established their reputation as loyal and gallant soldiers. It is strange that during those years the Nepalese nobility in Kathmandu still continued to play a fickle diplomatic game with the British, more often cold than warm in their attitude, more often than not intriguing with other chieftains against them, while down in India their mountain warriors served the hated rival. The intrigues which went on in the valley of Kathmandu caused many quarrels and invariably ended in bloodshed and atrocities, but these had little effect on the villages away in the hills, where the people, far from the horrors of the Royal Court, lived happy and contented lives. It is not surprising that these countrymen found common ground with the Englishmen who came out to India to soldier with them, sharing their love of field sports of all kinds. The early sahibs and their Gurkhas were mighty hunters. In the hill stations, at Dehra Dun, Almora and Abbotabad, there was a wide variety of wild game, with the rivers full of fish and unique opportunities for shooting in the hills. In such surroundings the British officers and their Gurkha soldiers built up a happy relationship to be cemented in time of war.

Not surprisingly, there are few authentic stories about the Gurkhas serving John Company during the period preceding the Indian Mutiny. That their attitude to hunting (*Shikar*) has not changed over the years is obvious. Brought up in a country where few of the mountain folk had the means to own firearms for hunting purposes, each round and every cartridge was something to be used with telling effect. For this reason the Gurkhas called ammunition *khajana* (treasure) and undoubtedly our Rifleman Manbahadur Limbu would have heard the phrase from his father, whose experiences on the North-West Frontier would have left a deep, abiding impression on him. To lose a round of ammunition or even abandon an empty cartridge case would have been considered a heinous crime, because to the warlike Pathans, ammunition was also 'treasure'—without which they could not feud with the British or, equally important, among themselves.

In illustration of this ingrained care of ammunition, live or spent, about a hundred years later Communist Terrorists launched an insurrection aimed at taking over Malaya. A platoon of Gurkhas was commanded by a young and very inexperienced British officer who, wisely, was leaving affairs to the Gurkha officer. When nearing the jungle edge, the platoon came under heavy fire which killed the Gurkha officer and a rifleman. The perilous situation was saved by a corporal who had won the Military Medal during the Second World War. Cool and unperturbed, the NCO organized a withdrawal, using covering fire and smoke to extricate the Gurkhas, section by section, who were exposed to view and a deadly fusillade of bullets.

As the last section doubled back, still under fire with the young and very shaken officer at their head, the corporal ran beside him and shouted, 'Sahib, do we have to pick up the empties?'

Even in adversity the corporal could not forget his days on the Frontier. And, of equal importance, that day the young subaltern learnt that to command such men demanded standards equal to, and above, their own—a big challenge indeed.

Though the majority of the hill tribesmen could not afford a shotgun and had to do their hunting with more primitive weapons, including the traditional national weapon, the kukri, the Nepalese nobility organized hunting on a large scale. From 1846 Nepal had a strong man at the helm, Jangbahadur Rana, whose rise to the dual post of Prime Minister and Commander-in-Chief had been meteoric and blood-stained. Jangbahadur, virtual dictator of Nepal until his death in 1877, dearly loved hunting and mounted huge expeditions, sometimes combining them with military manoeuvres down in the forests of the Terai. Jangbahadur was also a great Anglophile and the year he spent in the United Kingdom in 1850 induced him to take some long overdue steps towards modernizing Nepal. His admiration for Queen Victoria and her country heralded a dramatic change in Anglo-Nepalese relations.

In 1857 the flames of the Indian Mutiny threatened to engulf the tenuous British hold over India. With the passing of the years misconceptions about the Mutiny have grown, especially in the minds of modern Indian historians, supported by a few academics who seek to denigrate the British role in India. The temptation to present it as part of the struggle against the British, beginning in 1857 and ending in 1947, has proved difficult to resist. Nevertheless, definitive and authentic accounts written during and immediately after the Mutiny show that it was in fact a rising by parts of the Native Army as opposed to a national movement. Only in Oudh did it assume anything like the appearance of a national rising, affairs there having been brought to a head by tactless handling of much-needed land reform by the British officials concerned. Elsewhere the outbreak remained a military mutiny by sepoys, though they were supported by others who for various reasons sought to spread anarchy and destruction.

Few Indian princes thought that the English could win India back again but Jangbahadur was one of that handful; during his visit to Britain he had seen with his own eyes that the power of that small island did not rest on its few thousand soldiers and handful of administrators present in India. We must also remember that he had pledged his faith to Queen Victoria during his audience at Buckingham Palace, a pledge that was not given lightly. As a consequence, Jangbahadur threw the whole power of Nepal into the struggle on the British side and, among other things, permitted the East India Company to raise more Gurkha regiments. The first one raised was to be known later as the 4th Prince of Wales' Own Gurkha Rifles. At a later stage in the Mutiny Jangbahadur himself was to lead a contingent of over 6,000 soldiers down from his mountain kingdom to help General Sir Colin Campbell on the outskirts of the besieged town of Lucknow. Prior to that, however, the Gurkhas serving in the Company's Corps were to play an important part in the struggle which centred around Delhi. Briefly, we will follow the fortunes of these battalions before returning to the Nepalese contingent under Jangbahadur.

Even before the Mutiny broke out, the Gurkha soldiers, through one of their own officers, had asked to be allowed to pitch their tents with those of the British soldiers while on musketry courses at Amballa. The reason for this request was that they did not like being mixed up with the *Kala Log* (black folk), as they called the native sepoys whom they reported as showing, 'very bad feelings in their conversations regarding the use of the greased cartridges'. It was this which provided the spark that ignited the tinder of unrest: when the new greased cartridge was taken into service in the army, it was alleged to contain a proportion of cow tallow, odious to Hindus of every caste. Possibly also it contained pig fat, equally abhorrent to the followers of Mohammed. To Hindu and Moslem soldiers alike, who had to bite off the end of the cartridge to release the powder, it was an outrage to their religious feelings. Rumour spread that the British were deliberately trying to convert the sepoys to Christianity by making them lose caste. The Gurkhas, on this particular musketry course, requested that the greased cartridge should be given to them in order to show the Indian sepoys that they had no fellow-feeling with them on that particular question. A few days later, on 11 May, Bengal units of the Meerut garrison rose in armed mutiny.

On 14 May a tired camel sowar arrived in Dehra Dun with instructions that the Sirmoor Battalion was to move with the greatest possible urgency to Meerut where the Europeans were already in dire straits. The march to Meerut, even without opposition and considering the general chaos that existed in the countryside, was a test of endurance with distances of thirty miles a day being covered in the heat of the mid-May Indian summer, the soldiers wearing what today would be considered thick, unhealthy clothing. The first brush with the mutineers came on the fifth day near the Ganges Canal and some of the rebels were captured. The ringleaders were tried and shot that night; five of them were Brahmins, a good test of the many Brahmins then serving in the Sirmoor Battalion.

Fortunately for posterity, the Commandant, Major Charles Reid, wrote and retained letters throughout the march to Delhi and the siege that lasted for over four months thereafter; from him we learn how the struggle went until the final victory in mid-September. Even to reach Delhi entailed a considerable feat of stamina: the Gurkhas, marching through a night of terrific heat, covered twenty-seven miles before dawn the following day. After a short rest the men continued until they reached General Wilson's camp, dead beat and footsore, on 1 June.

Reid found that the British soldiers of the 60th Rifles were, in his words, 'knocked down by the sun and completely exhausted'. Nevertheless the whole force turned out and cheered the Gurkhas into camp but, as Reid wrote, 'my poor little fellows were so dead beat that they could not return the hearty cheers with which they were welcomed'. In spite of the initial warm greeting by their future comrades, the Gurkhas found that there was suspicion, trust in the other native regiments having been badly shattered by events in Meerut. As a consequence the Gurkhas' tents were pitched on the left, next to the artillery who, it was afterwards learnt, were to pound them if any signs of mutiny were detected. Events over the next few weeks were soon to dispel that initial mistrust and the highest degree of mutual admiration was attained.

It is not the purpose of this account to give details of historical events or attempt to describe the lengthy struggle for the city of Delhi. The Sirmoor Battalion, and some British comrades who fought alongside them, defended Hindu Rao's House, which owed its name to a former owner, a Mahratta nobleman. This strongly built mansion, together with a neighbouring observatory, provided accommodation and cover from fire for a substantial garrison and was to be the pivot of the British defences on the right flank of the Delhi Ridge. Shortly after Reid and his men had seized the House and its surrounds, the rebels mounted a fierce attack. Serving with Reid and his Gurkhas were two companies of the 60th Rifles, supported by guns from Scott's Battery, and in terrific heat they moved forward to meet and defeat the mutineers. The action took nearly sixteen hours and by that time the victors were utterly exhausted. For the Gurkhas their reward was to be cheered by the European troops on their return to the village in the evening; by now the soldiers of the Sirmoor Battalion were accepted as true brothers-in-arms by their British friends.

The mutineers did their best to persuade the hillmen to join their cause. A day or two later when Reid led his men forward, the rebels called out, 'Come on, come on Goorkhas; we won't fire upon you— we expect you to join us'. 'Oh yes,' was the reply, 'we are coming.' Thereupon the Gurkhas closed upon the centre of the rebels and when within twenty paces they gave the mutineers a well-directed volley, killing some thirty or forty of the 'scoundrels'—as Reid described them in his diary.

Throughout June, in the immediate pre-monsoon heat, Reid's small force was subjected to several attacks, often by as many as 8,000 rebels at a time. Charles Reid knew his men and, being no believer in static defence himself, realized that their morale would remain high if they were given the chance to close with the mutineers and wield their kukris in hand-to-hand conflict. On 15 June he wrote in his diary:

I gave the word forward; our little fellows were up like a shot and advanced in beautiful order to the top of the hill. By way of bringing the enemy on, I sounded the retreat having previously warned my men what we were going to do. It had the desired effect; on came the mutineers; we met just as I got over the brow of the hill. I gave them one well-directed volley and then ordered my guns to open. This sent them to a round-about and about fifty were killed and a great number wounded.

Mention has been made of the line boys, born and bred in the cantonments, and the part they played in this battle was notable. Of the twenty-five IOMs (Indian Order of Merit) given to men of the Sirmoor Rifles during the Siege of Delhi, twelve were won by line boys, the sons of serving soldiers: so much for doubts about their physique or courage. As an example, Reid relates:

I saw a boy squatting behind a rock with a rifle in his hands . . . He got up and saluted me, and said, 'I came here with the recruits. I have disobeyed orders, Sahib, but I could not help it. My father was on duty and I went there to assist him in getting out his cartridges. He was killed, and I then went to one of the 60th Rifles to help him in loading quickly. He was shortly afterwards wounded. He gave me his rifle and told me to get a doolie and send him to the hospital. I did so, and then went at it myself. After firing a few shots a bullet struck me which made four holes in my legs but I am not much hurt'. He looked quite pleased . . .

Reid enlisted the boy, although he was only fourteen, and sent him to hospital for treatment.

The Sirmoor Rifle casualties were mounting steadily, because, although the mutineers were not well led and tended to adopt the same tactics day after day, they fought with extraordinary tenacity. In his diary we learn from Reid that one little fellow, the best shot in the Regiment, Tikaran, died, adding that, 'He had killed twenty-two tigers in the Doon'. Unfortunately we have no more details about his exploits as a hunter. By this time Charles Reid was getting extremely concerned at the number of his 'little fellows' who had been killed or wounded, and only the timely arrival, at the end of July, of a draft of recruits and men returning from furlough saved the situation.

Charles Reid's admiration for 'my little fellows' was no greater than the opinions he expressed of the 60th Rifles under his command.

> The feeling that existed between the 60th Rifles and my own men was admirable: they call one another brothers, shared their grog with each other ... My men used to speak of them as 'Our Rifles' and the men of the 60th as 'Them Gurkhees of ours'.

This close fellowship and steel discipline was never to waver until the end of the siege, which came after a total of three months and eight days' continuous struggle. Near the end, the King of Delhi promised ten rupees for every Gurkha's head, the same price being offered for that of an English soldier. His wavering army was due to fight in front of the ladies of the city, seated in specially erected chairs and with the princes in attendance, dressed in green velvet suits covered with gold. Reid commented:

> His Majesty is coming out today to see his troops take my batteries and position. I shall be very happy to see him and only hope he will come out of the Moree Gate on the largest elephant he's got. A 24-pound shot would double up his Majesty, elephant, gold Howdah, and all!

The promised spectacle was the raising of the rebels' green standard over Hindu Rao's House. On the morning of the attack the King, attended by a large retinue and a number of his wives, came to the prepared place but the end was not as good as the beginning for the assault proved too costly and the royal spectators were forced to withdraw hurriedly into the city.

During the early days of August the long-awaited British reinforcements arrived under the command of Brigadier-General John Nichol-

son. Among these reinforcements was the Kumaon Battalion (later
1st Battalion of the 3rd QAO Gurkha Rifles), and despite a series of
forced marches at the height of the hot weather, the Battalion's
resilience was unimpaired. On 12 August they carried out a model
silent attack during which they took the mutineers' guns at Ludlow
Castle as well as killing a great number of the rebels who had been
surprised by the assailants' ferocity in assault.

The first meeting between Charles Reid and Nicholson, the 'Lion
of the Punjab', was not a happy one, the former disliking the General's
overbearing manner. But in time they became firm friends and
Nicholson was a frequent visitor to Hindu Rao's House, using
the observation post on the roof to gaze across at the mutineers.
Nicholson's experiences with the Gurkha sentries caused him, after
ten such visits, to demand of Reid: 'Why don't you instruct your
Gurkhas to let me pass? They've seen my face ten times now but still
they halt and challenge me.'

Just over a hundred years later a senior officer in the Brigade was
stopped by a Gurkha sentry who menacingly pointed a rifle and
gleaming bayonet at him when he was visiting his units during an
exercise on Salisbury Plain.

'Halt, who goes there?'

'Friend,' replied the Brigadier and started to move forward. Rifle
and bayonet were pointed even more aggressively at him.

'What is the password, friend?', and after a second's pause,
'Brigadier Sahib?'

Well known for his quick temper, the Brigadier said he didn't
know, adding, 'You know me, Rifleman Gopiram; I used to be your
CO.'

The Rifleman still kept his bayonet pointing at the officer but
grinned as he replied in a respectful manner, 'Yes, Sahib, I remember
you well but my platoon OC Sahib gave me a strict order: "No one
must pass who does not know the password—including the Brigadier
Sahib himself". That is what he said. So, I am obeying his order.'

By this time the Brigadier's face was as red as his headband and
there appeared to be an impasse. Fortunately the staff officer, who
was accompanying the Brigadier on the tour of inspection, saved the
situation by remembering the password himself. A visibly relieved
Brigadier stumped past the Rifleman who had done his duty. It was
the unfortunate Platoon Commander who was to catch the real blast
from the senior officer!

It must be remembered that the Mutiny was not confined to Delhi alone and the struggle was ebbing and flowing in various parts of India. Up in the Kumaon hills the 66th Gurkhas (soon to become the 1st Gurkhas) were part of a British force holding the town of Haldwani. Opposing them were two rebel forces, each of about 4,000 men with supporting guns, reported to be converging from different directions to make a combined attack on Haldwani. The Commanding Officer decided to defeat them in detail before they joined forces.

A force of about 500 men from the 66th Gurkhas, supported by two 6-pounder guns and a contingent of the Nepalese Army, marched all night through the forest and took the rebel army under Kali Khan by surprise at the village of Charpura. Heavily outnumbered though they were, the little force advanced against the enemy, the Gurkhas firing rapidly as they moved forward. Nothing could check such discipline under fire and the rebels fled. They then retraced their steps to Haldwani and, after marching thirty-four miles, arrived there after midday—all within the space of thirteen hours. In the event Haldwani was not attacked and, when the remnants of the rebel force trickled back to the town of Bareilly, their leader castigated them with the scathing denunciation: 'You worthless cowards! You took ten days to march from Bareilly to Charpura, only to come back in a matter of hours after seeing the British troops.' (He meant British-led Gurkhas and their fellow-countrymen in the Nepalese army.)

In the action the 66th Gurkhas lost a promising young officer, Lieutenant Gepp, and two men. After Lieutenant Gepp's death his parents gave the Regiment some of the letters he had written from 1855 until his death in 1858. As an ensign, frequently had he eulogized his Regiment: 'I am sure there is not a more celebrated corps in the world ... I fear you will be quite tired of hearing their praises sung but you must forgive my regimental esprit de corps.'

Back at Delhi on 14 September the grand assault began with Nicholson living up to his title of 'Lion of the Punjab' by being the first to mount the breach near the Kashmir Bastion. Waving his sword, he led those who took possession of the ramparts but tragically he was mortally wounded at the moment of his triumph. Behind him, the main body of the Kumaon Regiment (later the 3rd QAO Gurkha Rifles) drove the rebels from the Korwali and from Delhi's famous street, the Chandni Chauk, until it came up against the great mosque, the Jamna Masjid.

While they waited to storm the Kashmir Gate, another contingent from the Kumaon Regiment were witnesses to one of the most gallant feats in the Mutiny. A do-or-die party of eleven, commanded by Lieutenant Duncan Home of the Bengal Engineers, after crossing open ground under heavy fire, blew open the doors of the Gate. The Victoria Cross was awarded to four of the seven survivors— in those days the VC was not given posthumously. The main column, headed by the 52nd Foot, then poured through the Gate to win the day.

Reid's column, which consisted of about 2,500 men from various units, apart from his own Battalion, had some setbacks, particularly when the Commander himself was wounded. In the violent battle that followed, the defending sepoys fought stubbornly as the struggle ebbed and flowed. But, with clear objectives to strive for, the attackers slowly fought their way forward until organized resistance ceased, although bitter fighting was to continue in parts of the city until 16 September. Regrettably, vengeance was taken against the innocent as well as the guilty by the less disciplined members of the attacking army. On this point, Reid compliments the soldiers under his command for being forbearing in the heat of battle and at the moment of victory, a trait that they have invariably shown during the aftermath of many battles in subsequent campaigns.

The Mutiny did not come to an end when Delhi fell. It had received its death blow, but in various provinces disturbances still broke out; but we must now return to Prime Minister Jangbahadur Rana and his soldiers from Nepal.

The first contingent had marched from Kathmandu at the end of June and had driven out the mutineers from two or three towns in Northern India: the fortified position at Manduri was taken after five columns had swept into the fortifications erected by the mutineers and in a matter of minutes the defenders were fleeing from the highland warriors' kukris.

A few weeks later the fighting for the town of Chand was even more ferocious when the small force of Gurkhas, numbering about a thousand men, attacked an army some four or five times their number. Although suffering grievous losses themselves, the Nepalese assailants won the day, their particular hero being Lieutenant Gambirsing who, singlehanded, captured a gun after cutting down five artillerymen and wounding and driving away the others. We are told that he was covered with wounds but returned to fight again.

At such a moment did Lord Canning ask that the Prime Minister, Jangbahadur Rana, should move down into India at the head of the reinforcements which he had held ready for such a purpose over the previous four months. Jangbahadur responded with alacrity, being glad to leave Kathmandu, especially when there was a prospect of a fight. In retrospect, it was the most significant moment in the long history of friendship between Britain and Nepal; on to the world's stage stepped the short, stocky men who, over the next 130 years, were to die on many fields, invariably with honour, in battle against the enemies of their friends the British. Moving down to besieged Lucknow, where they joined General Sir Colin Campbell, the Nepalese contingent played a notable part in the series of attacks which led to the fall of that city. On 14 March, 1858, Jangbahadur's forces dispossessed the rebels of the outskirts of Lucknow, so his part in the campaign was now at an end.

The British did not forget such loyalty. The much-disputed strip of plain, running along the south of the Nepalese highlands, the Terai, was returned to Nepal to reward Jangbahadur for what he had done during those critical days. His soldiers had never seen such wealth as they saw in Oudh and, more especially, in the city of Lucknow. Loaded with plunder, the hillmen returned to their own country, followed by a baggage train of several thousand bullock carts, heavily laden with the loot collected during their year's campaigning. Although Colin Campbell complained at the amount of loot, he detached a special escort from his own regiment to help the Nepalese Army cross the border into the Terai.

Queen Victoria was to honour her ally, Jangbahadur Rana, with the Order and Jewels of the Knight Grand Cross of the Order of the Bath. In return, the Nepalese Maharajah promised that if ever the Queen or her Viceroy needed his services, they had but to ask, a pledge which was to be no idle one as subsequent years were to prove. Jangbahadur Rana reigned supreme in Nepal until, in February, 1877, he suddenly fell ill with fever and died. By the holy stream of the sacred river, Baghmati, his corpse was burnt and the three senior Maharanis committed 'suttee' on the pyre, a sacrifice that Jangbahadur would probably have forbidden. It is recorded that the senior Maharani, before she laid herself down to die in the flames by her dead lord, said:

Gentlemen, you all know of the love the Maharajah had for you and the zeal with which he devoted his life to the welfare of your country. If in the discharge of his duty he has ever by word, look or deed wronged any one of you, I, on his behalf, ask you to forgive him, and to join me in praying for the everlasting peace of his soul.

Thus passed the greatest ruler the country of Nepal has known in modern times. History will remember that the links he forged with the Royal Family and statesmen in London have stood the test of time, in bad days and in good, in peace and in war.

THREE

Volunteers A'Plenty

Gaining official permission to enlist volunteers into the Corps did not mean that thereafter recruiting was easily accomplished, especially in the early days, since no recruiting party was ever allowed to enter Nepal. As a consequence, the recruiters had to haunt the border villages in the hope of enticing young men, who had carried loads down to the plains of India as porters, into enlisting. A favourite time and place was a country fair where drink and other unaccustomed luxuries induced the hill youths to seek fame and fortune with the John Company. Recruiters roamed far and wide in their search for likely lads, going as far as Kumaon, where there were many Gurkha families who had continued to reside there since the days when that State had been occupied by the Nepalese at the end of the eighteenth century. From records, which are supported by old photographs, we learn that Garhwalis and Kumaonis of good stock were enlisted because it proved impossible to find enough Nepali recruits on the Indian side of the border.

The aftermath of the Mutiny led to much friendlier relations between those in authority in Kathmandu and the British Government and in the 1860s the military cantonment of Gorakhpore, conveniently near the Nepalese border, became the official centre for would-be recruits. In time appointed recruiters, all of them ex-soldiers, were allowed to return to their own villages and surrounding districts and shepherd volunteers down to Gorakhpore, journeys that took several days, sometimes even weeks, to accomplish. While British officers briefed these recruiters before sending them into Nepal, there was never any question of the British being allowed to venture into the country. This strict veto was to remain in force until the Rana regime collapsed after the Second World War, thus heralding the end of Nepal's isolation. The doors were opened to tourists and United Nations experts and Great Britain was allowed to establish recruiting depots on Nepalese soil in 1957, 140 years after the first Gurkha soldiers began serving the British.

A present-day soldier wrote in an examination: 'After the monsoon all soldiers are sent into the hills to enlist in the army. Their orders are to bring many young girls to the sub-depots.' He meant, of course, lads (*keta* as opposed to *keti*). How did the recruiter persuade these young men to leave their mountain homes? Some, and the percentage would vary from year to year, would leave with the blessings of their parents. In this case, before the would-be recruit left his house, his father might visit the local priest to see that the day of departure was auspicious. That having been settled, the boy would then set about bidding farewell to everyone in the village. The young man's salutations (*dhok*) to his senior relatives would be solemn and graceful, reminding any European observer that respect for elders in the hills was, and to a remarkable degree still is, similar to customs observed in royal courts in days gone by.

The boy's mother might give him a handful of small coins as he was about to leave and it is not unknown for the youth to give a coin to each of his girl-friends waiting along the route to garland him as their personal farewell. After such an organized emotional send-off, it is not surprising that many failed recruits did not wish to go back home, dreading the anticlimax of a return so soon after the heartfelt farewells.

But many would leave home like Sunbahadur Rai did in 1948. It began when a retired soldier appeared in the district and word got round that the British were looking for recruits in a hurry and in numbers. In Sunbahadur's case his resolve to enlist was strengthened when a friend and neighbour announced that he would come too. After a sleepless night the 16-year-old boy rose before dawn, leaving his few belongings in a neat and tidy fashion. He had not dared to tell his parents about his resolve; they would have forbidden him to go and, moreover, would have extracted a firm promise that he would not do so. After meeting his friend in the darkness they ran to the agreed rendezvous with the recruiter which they reached as the sun was rising. There a middle-aged man, his face half-hidden in a twisted muffler, came up to them and said hastily in their own Rai dialect: 'Are you two coming?'

'Coming, Huzoor,' said Sunbahadur.

'Good.' The recruiter looked anxious. 'Seen any others on the way?' The two lads shook their heads. 'Very well; that must be all.' It was then they saw that there was a group of young boys behind him. Sunbahadur counted twelve, the total that the recruiter was allowed to take into the depot. As it got lighter several of them recognized each other and soon found out that the majority had run away in pairs. All were farmers' sons and several had relatives who had served or were still serving in the army. A minute or two later the recruiter set off at a fast pace so that the boys had to concentrate on keeping up and not until nightfall did they halt at a lonely inn, far down the river, where they were obviously expected, since a meal of rice and fish was waiting for them in a shop. By now the twelve youngsters were almost too weary to eat. They had been up since well before dawn, they had walked or jogged miles to the rendezvous, had experienced the tension of running away from home, and had moved fast throughout the day with a few halts for rest and none for food. Next day they were heading for the recruiting depot.

After entering the depot, the recruiter, Bagbir Rai, formerly a sergeant in the 7th Gurkhas and now on pension, halted his group, arranged them in a rough line and duly reported to the recruiting officer. Thereafter the system took over, the bewildered boys being led to a store where each was issued with two blankets, a mess tin and a tin mug. Then to the cookhouse where, to their amazement, large enamel plates were filled with great ladlefuls of rice, split peas and mutton. The youngsters gulped it all down hungrily, before two of them rather doubtfully approached the cooks, who called out, 'Don't be shy' and filled their mess plates again.

Next day the actual recruiting would begin, the principles of which have changed little over the years, although with modern techniques such aspects as medical inspections have become much more thorough and efficient. For Sunbahadur and his friend—and indeed the group who accompanied them—the next two days were a considerable ordeal. They were weighed and measured; teeth and ears were examined; their chests were listened to by a British officer with tubes from his ears; Gurkha officers ordered them to run up and down the parade ground and watched their movements critically; and worst of all, as the weeding-out process continued, they were inspected not once but twice and then yet again by the senior recruiting officer.

The tension mounted as the youngsters stood still as stones, each wrapped in a blanket, until a Gurkha officer tapped them on the shoulder when they dropped the blanket to stand dressed in a pair of underpants only. (In years gone by it would have been a G-string.) Slowly the inspecting officers moved down the line, peering at each and every man with considerable care, speaking to them, testing their innate intelligence. Then it was Sunbahadur's turn. The Gurkha officer accompanying the British Recruiting Officer murmured:

'Too young, sahib, but we could take him next year.'

Sunbahadur's heart sank. His eyes pleaded with the British officer who mused to himself: 'Here is a youngster, a Rai, who has probably run away from home to join and unlike others around him—some a trifle old, others with a slight fault of posture or appearance—this lad's only fault is his youth.' Rarely did the Recruiting Officer disagree with his senior Gurkha adviser but on this occasion his instinct told him that Sunbahadur would become an excellent soldier. If he turned him down, then it was likely that the boy would not return home but seek employment elsewhere, down in the towns of India. The officer tapped Sunbahadur on the shoulder, murmured 'Front rank', and moved on.

For Sunbahadur the rest of the day passed like a wonderful dream, especially when he learnt that his friend had also been accepted. For the would-be recruits and their recruiter it had been a gamble, for the ex-NCO would only be paid for those in his charge who were accepted, a bonus being added for outstanding volunteers. For the failures the alternatives were a weary walk home or another journey to seek employment in India.

The recruiting depots are now on Nepalese soil and so methods have changed in recent years. Nevertheless, the ex-soldier recruiter is still at the heart of the matter; it is he who initially tours his own area and seeks out likely recruits. Clandestine meetings, plying unsuspecting youngsters with drink and other sharp practices are rarely necessary these days. With the annual recruiting targets for the British Army being very modest, the number of volunteers greatly outstrips the demand. The recruiters act as a sieve, the first process in the recruiting chain, before retired Gurkha officers (Assistant Recruiting Officers) eliminate all but those who come into the category of 'probables'. It is these only who trek down to Pokhara in West Nepal and Dharan in the East. Thereafter the system which Sunbahadur experienced comes into effect, with British officers taking the final decisions. This has to be, because considerable pressures are put on the retired Gurkha officers and pensioner NCOs, especially by those with whom there are close ties of blood or who have influence in their particular village or district. It is thus only fair that the very difficult decision as to whether to reject or accept the young hopefuls is taken by those who do not have to live in the community thereafter.

Tales told by recruiting officers abound and not surprisingly the majority of them concern the efforts of the young hopefuls to 'beat the system'. Advancing their age is the most obvious one—in contrast to those who are under the minimum weight which is something normally beyond their control. However, there have been several instances of likely youths who have volunteered for cookhouse duty and after a year of excellent feeding have changed from skinny lads weighing 85 to 90 pounds to well over the minimum limit and in the following year have presented themselves as strapping recruits. The wise British officers turn a blind eye to such goings on, knowing that extra labour for the Depot cookhouse is obtained with obvious benefits to the volunteer, but aware that the Command Secretariat would take a dim view of the extra mouths being fed 'on the house'.

How to gain weight in a hurry has posed a problem to many would-be recruits over the years. One man, desperate to be recruited but slightly underweight, was told to return the following morning. Overnight he took the precaution of drinking five pints of water and eating eight bananas; next day his weight was correct but so full was he that he could not expand his chest the required amount! Another young lad refused to take off his trousers when told to do so and be weighed in his underpants. When eventually he was persuaded that he would have no chance of being enlisted if he did not comply, he reluctantly stripped and there, strapped to his thighs, were two large stones, without which he would have been well under the required weight.

The recruiting staff have to be constantly on their toes, well aware that the longing to be enlisted overcomes any sense of fair play: the end justifies the means. The enlistment of underage recruits is not nearly as prevalent now as it was, especially during the two World Wars. Then the physique of the volunteer was deemed to be all-important. If he could withstand the rigours of training and cope with active service conditions, being under the age limit by a matter of months or even a year was not a vital factor as far as the recruiting officers were concerned. Moreover, many of the hopefuls genuinely did not know their ages. Nowadays the recruits are much better educated and, with citizenship papers, it is much easier to check on details which in the past were often a matter of conjecture.

Perhaps the most difficult period recruiting officers have ever experienced in modern times occurred just after New Year, 1948, when the four Gurkha regiments left India to join the British Army, initially to serve in Malaya. A few months before, the Indian Army Gurkha Brigade had been split into two, with the 2nd, 6th, 7th and 10th Gurkha Rifles being earmarked to serve HM Government, while the other six regiments were to remain behind as part of the refashioned Indian Army. After a considerable delay, during which rumours abounded and morale was inevitably shaky, all the men serving in the regiments selected to become British were given the chance to opt for one of three courses: to remain with their regiment as part of the British Army; to transfer to another Gurkha regiment, thereby remaining in the new Indian Army; or to go on discharge with some sort of compensation. While it was made clear to all ranks that the choice was to be made without any coercion there is no doubt that the men in most units were subjected to considerable pressure from the Viceroy Commissioned Officers (VCOs) and NCOs, particularly when the former had decided to 'opt' for India themselves. They then tried to justify a personal decision by taking many of the men with them.

When a Gurkha soldier said 'I will serve HMG', it signified that his association with the Indian Army had ended and also meant that he would be serving overseas permanently, something that had never happened before in peacetime. In one or two battalions the number of volunteers who opted for service with HMG was surprisingly low. As a result, early in 1948 there was a sudden demand for recruits to be enlisted in a hurry so that they could be sent to Malaya within a matter of weeks to build up the strength of the badly depleted battalions.

The recruiting system in being at that time entailed ex-soldiers, in receipt of Army pensions, being sent back into the hills about six months before the recuiting season was due to open. These recruiters would have been briefed about the numbers of recruits required, the minimum weight and height acceptable, and the dates by which they would have to bring them back to the depot. But in January, 1948, certainly at the Ghoon recruiting depot near Darjeeling, the situation was far from normal. The young captain who had to bear the load at the beginning described the problems he faced when told to set up a new HMG depot from scratch and virtually unaided.

In January, 1948, I had no recruiters on my pay-roll and no careful plan had been made to send information about recruiting into the most likely areas of East Nepal. In haste I selected two pensioner Gurkha Officers as my assistants and luckily one of them had some experience in recruiting during the war. I then sent these two old gentlemen to the local pension office and told them to bribe, cajole and persuade about thirty ex-soldiers to act as recruiters and return to the hills on our behalf.

We got our recruiters but inevitably they were a mixed bag; several inexperienced, some lazy and others unreliable, and a few first-class ones. The inexperienced brought back the most unlikely types as their contribution to our target of 450 recruits. The lazy never returned to Nepal but went into Darjeeling. Here they persuaded the local 'wide boys' to dress in hill clothing, briefed them about their adopted village in East Nepal and brought them up before me. The unreliable ones either didn't bother to bring anyone in at all or, if they did, they were accompanied by someone on the run from the police or his wife! And the few good ones worked wonders and just saved our venture from being a dismal failure.

I will never forget the long lines of young Gurkha hillmen drawn up for my inspection every morning. Shivering in the cold, they had to strip down for inspection and then each, wrapped in a blanket, waited for my verdict. Being inexperienced, I hated failing anyone, but my old Gurkha Officer kept me on the right lines. He soon spotted the 'spivs' dressed in Nepalese costume and sent them back to their normal jobs with a few caustic and well-chosen comments. He also bluffed those who pretended to come from the martial tribes by various pointed remarks about their mothers!

Now and again we were faced with a different sort of problem. A distinguished looking old pensioner would arrive, wearing a row of medals. With him would be his young son who had been educated in a Darjeeling school at great expense to his proud father. In some cases the boys were more Indian than Gurkha in appearance and habits and, anyway, we didn't want to enlist Indian-domiciled Gurkhas, but to have said so would have upset the old soldiers with years of loyal service behind them—so we evolved a more subtle plan.

We would provisionally accept the boy but mark on the list of men due for medical examination—'Doc; fail this chap, we don't want him'. Thus honour was satisfied and no one's feelings were hurt. The doctor was shocked when I first suggested this scheme but eventually understood that no Nepalese subject would write to the BMA about his duplicity!

The account reflects the inevitable chaos that continued until the recruiting organization was built up and properly established. The writer ends his story:

In the hurry and flurry we made mistakes, too many of them, I fear. Several serving soldiers had originally elected to remain with the Indian Army and not accompany the British Army Gurkha Regiments to Malaya. Then they had second thoughts after hearing glowing reports from those who had already risked their careers under the new regime! The rules were quite specific—those who'd already exercised their option to serve with the Indian Army were not allowed a second choice. However, it was not so easy to explain this, especially to soldiers who had served alongside us in the Second World War, but we did our best. We had no staff to check anything and undoubtedly some of these men re-enlisted, pretending to be raw recruits while others came up with fictitious British Army numbers and were sent off to Malaya. Eventually the Indian army posted them as 'deserters, believed to be serving in the British Army'. They were—and most of them were given a nominal punishment and allowed to stay.

My Gurkha officers quite enjoyed trying to sniff out these fellows after they had put on *pahari* (hill) clothing and did their best to behave like raw hill boys would. This required the connivance of the recruiter and no doubt small sums of money passed hands in their attempts to fool us, the recruiting officers. But however good actors they may have been, the problem was to keep it up, hour after hour, day by day, especially when a sudden shouted command at one of these gentlemen, who was bearing himself like a trained soldier, inevitably produced an instinctive reaction which gave the game away. Then they would pretend that they had served for a few days only in the Indian Army, without being officially enrolled as recruits. I found it all rather sad and have to admit now that on one or two occasions we looked the other way while one of our excellent wartime soldiers slipped through the net.

That account was written thirty-five years ago and it must be emphasized that such haphazard recruiting methods did not continue after the first few weeks, nor do today's RAMC doctors now fail would-be recruits for non-medical reasons.

Moving the depots into Nepal from the long-established centres on Indian soil inevitably revolutionized certain aspects of recruiting. As an example the British officers now know considerably more about the country from where their men are enlisted, knowledge that was previously culled from books or by patiently questioning soldiers about details of their homes. Now each year officially sponsored trekkers set off to visit traditional recruiting areas which are well known to a number of British officers. As internal communications within Nepal have improved so has it become easier for the recruiter and his band of hopefuls to reach one or other of the depots—Pokhara in the West and Dharan in the East. In certain areas it is even possible to travel by road in civilian buses or in one or two instances, to fly in the RNAC light aircraft—an expensive way of travelling and certainly beyond the pocket of potential recruits, unless they are sons of affluent senior Gurkha officers.

A distinguished ex-officer of the Brigade once remarked that recruiting can and does bring out some of the worst characteristics of the Gurkhas of Nepal. With an ever-increasing population and arable land becoming more and more precious in the hills, and gainful employment for the better educated members of society continuing to be hard to find, it is not surprising that pressures mount on the young men as they strive to gain one of the small number of vacancies available annually in Britain's Brigade of Gurkhas. If they are sons or relatives of pensioners, then their fathers, or elder brothers or uncles will do their utmost to get the boy into the Army, even if it means offering a bribe or exerting pressure on a pensioner working as a recruiter.

In the early 1970s it became clear that certain recruiters were finding it difficult to resist such pressures in their own villages, with one or two accepting bribes from rich neighbours to induce them to take their sons into the Depot as potential recruits. As a result, for two years an experiment was carried out whereby the bulk of the potential recruits came down from the hills unescorted, unsponsored and forced to pay all their own expenses to and from the Depot. During the first year the results could be said to justify the gamble but once the bush telegraph had spread the word, the following year the impracticability of the concept became apparent. An enormous number of applicants came pouring down: over 8,000 hopeful recruits came to one depot alone, over ten successive Fridays, and it was impossible to tell how many of these were local boys and how many of them reported more than once in the hope of being enlisted. It must be remembered that the 8,000 hopefuls were battling for a mere 150 vacancies. Not surprisingly, too, the small recruiting staff was swamped and even keeping a semblance of control proved to be a nightmare. So it was back to the traditional recruiting system—albeit with certain variations.

Today the recruiter brings his posse of hill lads to certain pre-arranged meeting places in the hills where they are vetted and weeded out by Assistant Recruiting Officers (AROs, all ex-QGOs). In order to alleviate pressures, another experiment was introduced into the way hill selections were made wherein no ARO was sent back to his own district nor did he know where he and his senior rank escort were going until a week before the notified date. 'At last, life is bearable,' observed one distinguished ARO, words that summed up the considerable pressures exerted on even the most senior ex-Gurkha officers by their fellow villagers, and to a greater degree by their relations.

Nowadays pensioner Gurkha officers (AROs) have to visit the hills on two occasions each year, firstly to prepare for recruiting by advertising the dates and places where they plan to see anyone keen to join the Army, and secondly, a few months later, to choose their potential recruits and to brief the recruiters who are to escort the volunteers down to one or other of the depots at a later date. Now it is widely understood that there is no profit in bribing a recruiter because he cannot conduct anyone without having an ARO's pass. At the depot the selection process, covering $4\frac{1}{2}$ days, tests each young man's character, physique and mind. Some of the older members of the Brigade will cast their minds back to years gone by when recruiting was very much a cattle mart: if a boy looked right and came from the right background he was taken, with scant regard to his scholastic achievements which, in those days, would have been virtually nil anyway.

At the time of writing (1983), potential recruits undergo a series of selection tests and checks which include: a check on their citizenship which is confirmed by producing the correct document; Intelligence tests, which are done twice; Nagri literacy and numeracy tests; a physical assessment by Gurkha and British recruiting officers, including a one-mile run and certain physical efficiency tests; medicals, which nowadays include chest X-rays and audio metric tests; lengthy interviews by British and Gurkha Recruiting Officers; and final selection and inspection by the senior British Recruiting Officer.

With the very different type of training the soldier in the British Army now has to undergo, it is vital that recruits are capable of absorbing a mass of education, military instruction and other knowledge and in a much shorter time than in years gone by. For example, the recruits have to start specialized signals, engineering or driving courses within months of being enrolled in the Army. A different type of recruit is therefore required, but this does not make the task of the British Recruiting Officers any easier, especially when they have to reject fine young hill boys from the more distant parts of the mountains of Nepal, merely because they are almost illiterate. Unfortunately the modern Brigade does not have the time to educate those who cannot read or write to the required standard during the basic recruit course and more and more are the vacancies being filled by those who have moved down with their parents from the hills to settle in Kathmandu, Pokhara or in the Terai, where life is easier and there are schools readily available—schools that can be reached by bus as opposed to a two-hour walk each way, as is the case in many mountain villages.

There have been many changes, but one thing remains today as it has done since 1815: volunteers seeking enlistment always greatly outstrip the small annual demand. Some left-wing politicians in Kathmandu may resent the fact that their countrymen continue to serve the foreign armies of India and Britain but to date they cannot suggest an alternative solution. Nepal needs the money sent home by her Gurkha soldiers, which adds up to a considerable sum each year, one that could not be replaced from within Nepal itself which has few resources outside tourism—and her splendid hill warriors.

FOUR

The North-West Frontier

Between 1878 and 1947 officers and men serving in the Indian Army Gurkha Brigade were constant visitors to the bare hills and mountains of the North-West Frontier. The Frontier posed a problem which the British never resolved and, although numerous punitive expeditions were launched, in addition to the three Afghan Wars during the period, the unbending tribesmen retained a sturdy independence, fuelled by pride in their religion and race. As an observer wrote in 1908:

> Their bearing proud and apt to be rough. Inured to bloodshed from childhood, they are familiar with death, audacious in attack, but easily discouraged by failure. They are treacherous and passionate in revenge.

During this period British statesmen were highly sensitive to Russia's blatantly displayed ambitions in Afghanistan. Now, with the benefit of hindsight, it is easy to understand that the Russians had equal grounds for suspecting the motives of the British as they moved north-west through the Punjab to reach the mountains which separate India from Afghanistan. These mountains were a barrier to the soft-hearted but a home for the Pathans who greeted the encroachment into their territory with suspicion and hatred. Relations with Afghanistan were always delicate and inconsistent British policies heightened the sense of insecurity which kept the pot boiling along the Frontier.

Although there was never any love lost between the adversaries on the Frontier, it is only fair to state that the British political agents who lived among the Pathans, the Wazirs or Mahsuds, speaking their tongues and knowing their customs, took a more lenient view of their peoples' transgressions; indeed, there were several recorded instances of the agents talking about 'our fellows doing well', following an encounter with British or Indian troops. Such remarks did not endear these gentlemen to the regiments concerned after the action was over.

That there was a mutual respect between the Gurkha soldiers serving in the Indian Army and the tribesmen is all too evident from various accounts contained in the Brigade's regimental histories. However, the Gurkha's high regard for their foe was in no way tempered by affection, because their enemy rarely, if ever, showed mercy; prisoners in their hands seldom survived to tell the tale and some of the atrocities the tribesmen—and their womenfolk—carried out were horrible in the extreme. Dead bodies of their adversaries, be they Indian, British or Gurkha, were usually mutilated in a bloodthirsty fashion. For this reason the soldiers operating on the Frontier made every effort to recover fallen comrades. To get all the wounded away was a point of honour on the Frontier, even if to recover a single man meant that a full-scale counter-attack had to be mounted by the rearguard. It is easy to understand why the Gurkhas frequently had to be restrained by their British officers from retaliation against captured Pathans.

Against such a relentless foe the soldiers knew that they could never relax for a single moment; keen hostile eyes watched their every movement, seeking chinks in defences and probing for tell-tale signs of slackness or ill-discipline. A moment's relaxation could mean death or the loss of a valuable weapon or equally vital ammunition. To lose a weapon through negligence was considered a terrible disgrace. In one regiment a Gurkha *havildar* (sergeant) hung himself after losing his rifle to a tribesman. Another example of such ingrained discipline, even when near death, has been recounted by a retired officer. In 1940 a young rifleman was hit and mortally wounded in the chest by a sniper and, cradled in the officer's arms, the dying youngster spoke his last words. At death's door the Gurkha's first call was to find out whether his rifle was safe and had not fallen into enemy hands; his second was a prayer and his last an appeal for his wife to be looked after by the *paltan* he had tried to serve with loyalty.

Campaigning in such a country was never easy, since nearly every village was capable of becoming a temporary fort and potential enemies were everywhere; movement along the roads was a slow, laborious business—'bullocks endeavouring to tread down wasps'—

which entailed piquets being sent up to the heights, the scaling of which required a high standard of physical fitness and considerable agility from the troops concerned. Moreover, even when the piqueting was carried out efficiently, there was always a definite risk when the time came to pull back the small force, often under pressure from the tribesmen. Men on piquet duty had to withdraw at speed, using what little cover there was while they scampered down to rejoin the main column below. The Gurkhas were in their element, possessing the ability to descend in great crashing bounds, leaning forward down the slope, their legs going as fast as in a sprint; it was something that even the Pathans could not surpass. To this very day the Brigade of Gurkhas hold an annual 'Khud Race' in the New Territories of Hong Kong and the speed with which the Gurkha runners leap their way down the steep rocky mountain fills British spectators with an awe approaching disbelief. Hence the remark passed by a British soldier after his incredulous friend had said, 'Gor, look at them wot's coming down the hill.'

'Yeah, they ain't human, are they?'

Years after the Brigade had ceased to operate on the North-West Frontier, the pilot of a Scout helicopter was flying near the Hong Kong–Chinese border when he saw three Gurkha soldiers with heavy loads at the foot of Kong Shan Hill. The pilot, who had close links with the 7th Gurkhas and was subsequently to carry out an extended secondment tour with them, decided to land, and offered to ferry them and their kit up the hill—an offer which was gratefully accepted. Determined to impress them and by using full power, he hurtled the Scout up to the top in 30 or 40 seconds. As the grateful Gurkhas were getting out, the pilot said to the senior one, a sergeant: 'I bet even Corporal Rukman Limbu (the Brigade Khud Race champion) couldn't get up the hill as fast as that!' Quick as a flash the NCO replied, 'No, Sahib, but he doesn't need petrol.'

Operations on the Frontier demanded a thorough knowledge of the various drills which had been worked out to combat the mobile and lightly armed tribesmen. Not surprisingly, the British and Indian Armies considered it an excellent training ground for war, with live bullets instead of 'blanks' being used, while the leadership of junior officers and NCOs was tested under conditions of real stress and danger. Awards for gallantry were granted, which acted as an incentive for the Gurkhas, who tend to set high store on 'gongs'. Many of those who have been awarded a decoration subsequently sign their

names with the decoration immediately after their signature. Recipients of gallantry medals are invariably called within the unit or sub-
unit concerned, 'MC Sahib'—if a Gurkha officer—or 'MM' if another
rank. Back in their villages, the holders of gallantry medals are treated
with great respect because until the end of his days the award adds to
the local prestige of the recipient. Most of the males living in the
village will be able to describe how the award was won, no doubt as
a result of hearing the story several times from the holder over a glass
of *raksi* (rum) at night. The majority of Gurkhas have a charming
lack of false modesty but at the same time they rarely, if ever, boast
about their exploits.

Stories about Gurkhas on the Frontier inevitably include a few
bloodthirsty incidents, some of which, no doubt, are apocryphal.
There were moments of humour, too, as the tales of two buglers, in
different regiments, illustrate. A light-hearted story comes from the
1st Gurkha Rifles, written by the then Lieutenant Ryder (later to
retire as a Colonel).

We were actually ordered to capture a piquet as it was essential to
secure a prisoner in order to get information. I remember the
stalking of the piquet well, as it was exciting and took a long time,
and to do it we had to get well into the enemy's country. At one
critical moment, when we were all lying on our faces on the wet
stones and moss quite close to the 'Sangar' we were stalking, the
bugler, whose name I forget, suddenly started a violent fit of
coughing. He was violently kicked and punched by those nearest
him, and in despair he turned his bugle mouthpiece into the wet
ground and started coughing into the broad end. The sounds he
got out were startling, but luckily the enemy never heard him. Our
medical officer came with me on this little show, just to see the fun,
and I am sure he enjoyed it as much as anyone.

It is appropriate to follow that with another story about a bugler.
Early in the 1920s a Gurkha battalion was serving at the end of the
Khyber Pass near the Afghanistan border. It so happened that the
Brigade Commander and the CO of that battalion were not very fond
of each other. One day when the Brigade commander passed the
battalion's lines, the Quarter Guard turned out to pay him the
customary compliments due to his rank, accompanied by a salute on
the bugle. When the NCO in command of the guard gave the order,

the guard smartly and quietly presented arms from the 'order' while the bugler attempted to blow his bugle, standing on the left of the guard. To his great embarrassment he found that his usual blow had no effect. In desperation he blew again much harder, whereupon, to the accompaniment of a faint noise, a packet of 'Scissors' cigarettes and a box of matches flew forth to land at the feet of the astonished Brigade Commander, watched by an equally surprised staff officer.

The nature of the subsequent complaint received by the CO of the Battalion from the Brigadier and the punishment meted out to the erring bugler have not been recorded for posterity.

The Gurkha's natural hunting instincts are never completely submerged by training and military discipline and may suddenly come to the fore, even when their minds should be on other things. On one occasion when two companies of the 4th Gurkha Rifles were on the Frontier, 'B' Company was startled by a volley of shots from 'A' Company which came whistling over their heads. In those days there were no wirelesses and flags were used for communications. In a flash 'B' Company's flags spelt out a query to find out what was happening, only to learn that the shots had not been aimed at tribesmen but at wild game. An oorial, a species of mountain sheep, bewildered by the firing, thereupon trotted back into the middle of the battle. Both companies forgot about the human enemy—and also about each other—and opened fire at the fleeing animal. A senior Gurkha officer hit the oorial while it was galloping at full speed at a range of over a hundred yards. One or two ex-officers sent in similar stories, describing how smartly dressed recruits were standing rigidly to attention until their recently acquired discipline disappeared dramatically when a hare or other wild animal bolted across the parade ground. In a flash the majority of the recruits broke rank, shouting 'Ayo, ayo', and charged hither and thither in an attempt to corner the frightened animal.

Shooting of wild game has continued over the years; it is an instinctive reaction of any Gurkha soldier. During the Italian campaign of the Second World War, some officers were having a quiet cup of tea in the Mess lorry at a brigade headquarters. Suddenly bullets came whizzing over their heads which caused them to hit the floor without ceremony. A *naik* (corporal) was detailed to take four men and deal with the German sniper who had upset their tea break. Eventually the *naik* returned and was asked if he had dealt with the unfriendly German.

'No; it wasn't a German sniper; it was the 2/8th Gurkhas shooting chickens.'

Such events are unlikely in the built-up New Territories of Hong Kong but the hunting instincts remain, even if today's recruits are more sophisticated than their forbears.

One thread appears to be common to the majority of the Frontier stories: the agility and the incredible speed shown by the Gurkhas when faced with the steepest of cliffs or confronted by the most dangerous of ravines. Nevertheless, it was never a one-sided encounter and all battalions learnt much from their enemy. They came to appreciate the value of unwinking, unsleeping alertness. The Pathans showed them how to use ground tactically, reminding them that the penalty of carelessness was death. They came to respect the tribesmen even if they never grew to like them. On being faced with the Japanese in Burma during the 1945 war, and after resisting an attack against great odds, a subedar shook his head before saying to his British officer, 'If the Japani-haru were Pathans, we'd have had a very bad time, Sahib.' A high compliment, especially at a time when most of the Allied soldiers were treating the Japanese soldiers as if they were supermen.

Before the Second World War life on the Frontier varied from station to station. One retired officer recalls what it was like when his battalion moved to Chaman on the Baluchistan frontier with Afghanistan which he described as 'a veritable pre-war Indian Aldershot. For recreation there was tennis, squash and golf'. Moreover, during his tour there, ladies were allowed in the Mess for the first time, thus contravening one of the strictest rules in the Indian Army military code.

> The Commandant took pity on the ladies and permitted the married officers and their wives to dine in the Mess every night.... I do not recall why the Commandant permitted this relaxation of the rule except that it was very difficult to get servants to come out from Quetta so perhaps that was the reason.

Unfortunately for this young subaltern and one of his fellows, they were inveigled into making up a bridge four with the Second-in-Command and his wife who were both extremely keen and excellent players. Husband and wife always partnered each other, a formidable combination as the two press-ganged subalterns found out every night for the six months they played. 'By the end I never wished to see a bridge table again and to this day I am very wary of admitting I play.'

One peculiar duty that had to be carried out was the inspection of the Khojak Tunnel on the railway. A few years before, Quetta had suffered a devastating earthquake and stringent precautions had to be taken thereafter. One of the company commander's duties was to inspect the railway tunnel at least twice a day by riding through it on a man-powered trolley supplied by the station master, who generally went along for the ride. To complicate movement within the tunnel, the track rose quite sharply to approximately the half-way point before dropping for the second half. The officer and the station master sat like overseers on the trolley with only hurricane lamps for light while four sweating coolies pushed them up through the gloom until a chink of light appeared. As this gradually enlarged and the trolley crossed the rise, the coolies jumped on the accelerating trolley, whereupon the whole party went hurtling down the incline with only the trolley brakes to stop them going all the way down to Chaman. Then the process had to be repeated in reverse.

Life in Chaman itself was very different to the conditions that greeted the columns whenever they moved out into the country on operations against the marauding tribesmen. Cruel though the Frontier often was, many of those who served there look back with nostalgic yearning. An ex-officer wrote:

I would give a lot to hear just once more the quiet commands on the parade ground, the muffled jingle of the mules' harness and their stamping on the yak as the yak-dans were loaded, and to see again the bright stars in the brittle night air recede into the crisp dawn light as the sun rose in splendour just behind the distant white peaks.

Whether his Gurkha soldiers would have agreed with all those sentiments is debatable. Professor Sir Ralph Turner, while serving in the fort at Thal, wrote a poem about the North-West Frontier in which he depicts a Gurkha sentry dreaming about his beloved Nepal—oblivious to the harsh grandeur around him.

His eyes saw: yet he noticed not: for all his thought
was in his own far country and in fancy sought

A hillside village and a sounding waterfall
Midst the green glory of deep-forested Nepal.

Alas, few would describe modern Nepal as being deep-forested but
we would be happy to follow the homesick sentry's soul as,

Hastening o'er hill and plain and sandy river-bar
On the strong wings of memory was gone to seek
The sun-lit dawning on a far Himalayan peak.

FIVE

The Warriors Step on to the World Stage

Although many would claim that the modern-day Gurkha soldier is as good as, or even better than, his forbears, no one can dispute that it was the two World Wars which established his reputation as a soldier. The great Maharajah, Jangbahadur Rana, forged the first links during the Mutiny; some fifty years later, another notable Prime Minister, Maharajah Chandra Shamsher Rana, did not hesitate when his friends, the British, went to war with Germany.

Although not a flamboyant personality like his illustrious predecessor, Chandra did much to foster the friendship between his country and Great Britain. He came to power in 1901 and soon proved himself a benevolent autocrat who introduced much-needed reforms in his backward kingdom. In particular, Chandra was determined to abolish slavery which was still rampant in the hill tracts of Nepal. It was to take much patience and infinite skill before he achieved his aim. Drink was another of his targets and the measures taken by him were to help resolve one of the national failings; yet another was gambling, which he tackled by forbidding the giving of credit to the loser.

So fierce was the average Gurkha's love of gambling that the great Jangbahadur had passed a law that gambling would be only permitted officially once a year, at the festival of Dewali when the sport started on the beat of a drum. Thereafter until the end of Dewali all else was, and still is, thrown aside while the majority of the male population gives itself up to gambling.

The cornerstone of Chandra Shamsher's policy was his steadfast friendship with Great Britain. In 1908 he went to England where he was given an enthusiastic reception. The warmth of the greetings that

met the Maharajah led him to write this letter of thanks to the British
people:

> Wherever we have gone we have found everyone anxious to make
> us feel that we were friends ... I want to and do thank the British
> people for all their kindness ... Yours is a great country ... But to
> me the greatness of your country is best seen in the good that is
> done for our great neighbour, India, in the peace, security of life
> and property, justice and numerous other benefits it has given to
> that country. So I take my leave, with the wish that God may
> prosper the people of this country and their work, and by again
> saying how much I and my people have enjoyed the kind hospitality
> which has been so fully extended to us and for which we are all so
> thankful.

Such words should be remembered by those who denigrate the British
and the way they governed their Indian Empire. The newly-crowned
King George V visited India in 1911 and at Chandra Shamsher's
invitation went on one of the biggest shooting expeditions ever
organized in Nepal. Records show that the British King, one of the
best shots of his day, accounted for twenty-one tigers, ten rhinoceros
and two bears—a bag that would make him the prime target of the
anti-blood sport crusaders of today! There was a genuine rapport
between the British King and the Maharajah and after the visit, the
King sent the message: 'Dear Maharajah, I can always count upon
you and your people as my truest friends.'

Three years later such words were translated into action with an
alacrity that surprised friend and foe alike. The little nation, which
at that time boasted a population of less than five million people, was
to send over 200,000 of its manhood down from the mountains to
fight for a King-Emperor they had never seen and who lived across
the 'Black Water'. With remarkable speed the ten regiments of the
Gurkha Brigade were expanded, as newly-raised wartime battalions
joined their regular counterparts. The Prime Minister of Nepal's
generous pledge to give help to his British friends encouraged and
influenced young men into joining the British-Indian Army.

But the Maharajah did more than just allow his young hillmen
to join the Indian Army. Four Nepalese Army regiments were
despatched to the North-West Frontier of India, a further six being
sent to carry out internal security duties in North India; over 16,000

men of Nepal's own army served in the garrison of India and, by keeping the peace, relieved the British and Indian battalions to go overseas.

Between 1914 and 1918 the soldiers of the Gurkha Brigade fought and died in France and Flanders, Mesopotamia, Persia, Egypt, Gallipoli, Salonica and Palestine. During those years they were to gain a worldwide reputation as first-class soldiers. Although having to fight in the trenches of France under conditions of climate and warfare unknown to them, the Gurkhas earned high praise from General Sir James Willcocks, commanding the Indian Corps, when he wrote, 'I have now come to the conclusion that the best of my troops in France were the Gurkhas . . . Taciturn by nature, brave and loyal to a degree, the Gurkhas ended, as I knew they would, second to none.'

Although the bitterly contested campaign in Gallipoli ended in failure, the Commander-in-Chief, General Sir Ian Hamilton, was to write at the onset: 'Each little Gurkha might be worth his full weight in gold at Gallipoli'. General Hamilton was not to change his opinion and when the campaign was over his secretary later wrote in this vein to the 6th Gurkhas: 'It is Sir Ian Hamilton's most cherished conviction that had he been given more Gurkhas in the Dardanelles then he would never have been held up by the Turks.'

Prior to the Gallipoli campaign the Indian Corps had been in France. When the 1/4th Gurkhas arrived at Marseilles in the heart of a severe European winter, they were given new machine guns and rifles and issued with warm clothing. The men were highly pleased with the woolly vests and long drawers with which they were issued. Indeed, they pulled them on over their thin khaki uniforms and, thus arrayed, marched the half-mile from the clothing depot back to the ship. This unrehearsed display caused a great sensation among the ladies of Marseilles who turned out in force to behold the strange spectacle.

On that day they may have been figures of fun, but, thrown into the winter trenches of France, ill-clad, ill-armed and faced with a fully-equipped German army, while they suffered fearful losses they still administered a smart beating locally to their opponents during several of the early battles—at Givenchy in 1914 and later at the battle of Neuve Chapelle. In 1915 the first Gurkha soldier won the Victoria Cross, an award which had already been won by British officers serving with the Gurkha Brigade, but not by any of the men since they were not hitherto eligible for the award. Rifleman Kulbir Thapa of the 3rd Queen Alexandra's Own Gurkha Rifles, himself wounded, found a badly wounded soldier of the 2nd Leicestershire Regiment behind the first-line German trench and, though urged by the British soldier to save himself, remained with him all day and night. In the early morning of 26 September, in misty weather, he brought him out through the German wire and, leaving him in a place of comparative safety, returned and carried in two wounded Gurkhas, one after the other. Kulbir then went back in broad daylight for the British soldier and brought him in, carrying him most of the way and being at most points under the enemy's fire. The foregoing is a precis of the citation which apeared in the *London Gazette*. It is interesting to note that the first VC won by a Gurkha was given because he saved the lives of his fellow soldiers, instead of killing the enemy during close-quarter fighting with his kukri, which many would have anticipated.

Professor Sir Ralph Turner, who as a young man was to win the MC serving with the 3rd QAO Gurkhas during the First World War, translated a Gurkha poem entitled *The Song of France 1914–1915*. Ralph Turner in time became Director of the School of Oriental and African Studies and was to produce the comprehensive *Comparative and Etymological Dictionary* of Nepali. The poem is too long to be quoted in full but some extracts are reproduced below.

When I reach Marseilles I cannot count the ships of the sea. Shall we live to return to India? That I cannot say.

Terrible was the German attack through the shafts of Debi. For three years my soul exalted in the fight.

The English soldiers came hot-foot to the land of France. The rain of bullets speeding night and day, our hearts weep bitterly.

In the land of France in the month December fell snow. Falling in battle my brothers died by the curse of Kali.

The land of France is cold and biting. I put on my greatcoat. Obeying the order I attacked and slew the Germans.

The shells of the guns coming like fine rain give greeting; on their backs and on their faces my friends and brothers die—shall any count them?

Carrying my friend and brother my body has been wetted with drops of his blood.

In France thus daily they were killed by the guns of the enemy.

When my body was weak and despaired, then came fever. In the
houses of France I found no refuge from the peril of bullets.
The rain has come pouring, I will put on my greatcoat. The shells
of the gun come quickly; where shall I go to hide?

The soldier-poet ends by saying: 'Be not a coward; die in battles; do
not despair.'

Those words which, notwithstanding Ralph Turner's skilful and
faithful translation, lose some of their impact in English, mirror the
fatalism of the average Gurkha soldier. The horrendous conditions
in the trenches would have done nothing to dispel such feelings,
especially when the bulk of the casualties were inflicted by shell and
bullet, fired by an unseen enemy.

Another First World War incident took place when the 4th Gurkhas
relieved the 1st Devons as part of the Suez Canal defence force. In
the customary way, the men took their guard duties seriously. One
party, consisting of an NCO and a section, was stationed on the Canal
with orders to fire on anything approaching their post that they
thought dangerous. One evening, we are told, a British battleship was
coming down the Canal. The Adjutant received a telephone message
from the NCO at his post near the Canal: 'Sahib, there is a big ship
covered with guns coming down the Canal; shall we fire?' Later the
Adjutant asked the man at what part of the ship he would have
directed his section's fire. 'Oh, at the Captain Sahib and the other
sahibs on the bridge,' replied the NCO with shrewd common sense.

The story got around naval circles and thereafter, before any British
battleship or cruiser moved through the Canal, an urgent message
would arrive from the Senior Naval Officer, 'HMS *Blank* coming
down the Canal; for God's sake tell your men not to fire.'

Another variation of the same story—it could be apocryphal—tells
us that a British destroyer was challenged by a small voice which
shouted from the land to the officer on watch words that sounded
like, 'Halt! Who-go-dah?' The accepted version goes on to allege that
the officer did not reply, whereupon a second challenge induced the
officer to switch on a searchlight which lit up one solitary Gurkha
rifleman standing on the bank, his rifle aimed at the side of the ship.
Thereafter, there seem to be two different endings to the story. One,
which seems a trifle unlikely, maintains that the destroyer stopped
until a British officer of the Gurkhas was found who could tell the
sentry that the ship could pass, which it did after a traditional 'Pass

friend: all's well'. The other variation maintains that the gallant little sentry was forced to open fire at the ship, his bullets making a harmless but resonant 'ping-ping', but nevertheless causing great consternation. Whatever may or may not have happened, certain it is that Gurkha sentries stood guard beside the Suez Canal and no doubt the Royal Navy was challenged on more than one occasion.

The ability of Gurkhas to get on with other races has been mentioned before and in illustration there is a little story about the people of a French village, Locon, who had never seen Indian or Gurkha troops before, and, not unnaturally, were inclined to resent the idea of them being billeted locally. One British officer came back to a farm expecting to find strained relations between his men and the farmer with whom they were billeted, as the man had been openly hostile during the officer's first visit. To his surprise he found their host all smiles, telling the Gurkhas to take what straw they wanted and, after apologizing for his former hostility, said that the Gurkhas had found several eggs in his barn and had brought them to him. 'Your men must be very good men; if they had been French *poilus* they would not only have kept my eggs but would be cooking and eating my chickens by now.' Being farmers themselves, and generally impecunious ones at that, their reluctance to help themselves in that situation can be understood.

Another story from France tells us that a little old French lady locked up her barns and positively refused to have them occupied, in spite of a British officer trying to persuade her. Losing patience, the officer told his subedar that he had better break open the barns and occupy them, but the Gurkha officer asked permission to arrange matters in his own way. Half an hour later when the British officer returned he found the old lady smiling and happy, busily serving out clean straw to his men and doing all she could to make them comfortable. As to the subedar, by this time he had a room to himself, with a feather bed and clean sheets, and was seated in an easy chair by the fire drinking hot coffee. Wisely, the officer did not ask any questions and never knew how the matter had been arranged so satisfactorily.

Some thirty years later, in the Second World War, a similar situation occurred in Italy when two British officers were refused permission by an Italian Contessa for two of the bottom rooms of her palazzo to be used by the officers of the company. In chagrin they went off to drink some *vino* in a local café where half an hour later the company clerk came to tell them that the Contessa had relented; indeed, three rooms had been given for their use. The company clerk spoke excellent Italian, which, his officers suspected, had been picked up during several short liaisons with 'ladies'. Now he was told to find the Contessa and relay their gratitude to the lady. He was not seen again until the small hours of the morning when one of the officers returned to the palazzo after checking the sentries at the other end of the village. The company clerk was tiptoeing downstairs from the Contessa's bedroom, dressed in his underpants, with a satisfied look on his face. Nothing was said at the time but his movements thereafter were watched with more than a little suspicion, and it must be added, a degree of envy on the part of his non-Italian-speaking officers!

From dalliance back to war. When the Royal Marines 'yomped' across wild inhospitable country in the Falklands, quite rightly the feat was acclaimed throughout the world. Nevertheless such distances would have meant little to the soldiers of the First World War. In the terrific heat of Mesopotamia the 1st Gurkhas carried out a forced march from near the Shumram crossing to Baghdad, some hundred miles; the going was very bad and the troops suffered greatly from ulcerated feet. The CO later wrote: 'I have never seen greater pluck displayed than during that march. Not a man fell out, although I used to see the blood actually oozing out of their boots. Many of their feet were fearfully ulcerated and in a terrible condition.'

The Gurkha's legendary toughness can be illustrated over and over again in stories from the First World War. At the Battle of Sharon in 1918 we are told that the one unwounded Gurkha picked up a Lewis gun and carried it, as well as 376 rounds of ammunition, until he eventually joined another section and was able to share his burden with the other men. This ability to bear extraordinarily heavy, unwieldy loads stems from their background, where even the smallest children are expected to shoulder their share of the burden, which they do in baskets on their backs, supported by a headband around their foreheads. From there they graduate to carrying weights which the average European would find difficulty in lifting off the ground, let alone being able to carry over rough ground, or up and down steep gradients which would tax one's balance and lung-power even without a load.

As a result of their fighting record during the early months of the First War, the British public had begun to take 'Johnny Gurkha' to their hearts. Such admiration caused Mr E. Foster to write on 15 November, 1914:

> Dear Gurkhas, we most heartily thank you for your great services you have rendered to England during this Terrible Trial in which we are placed but not through our seeking; may God protect you all and give you a safe and speedy return to your homes and beloved ones, kindly let me have a little note; signed E.F.

Like all units which served in the trenches between 1914 and 1918, the Gurkha battalions of the Indian Corps suffered terrible losses. It was for such a reason that this gesture of gratitude for their sacrifices was received from Pulford & Sons, the regimental tailors in St James's Street, London, demonstrating that even regimental tailors can be swayed by sentiment.

> Sir
> We beg to acknowledge your favour of the 24th instant and herewith forward ribbons as requested, trusting the same will be found satisfactory. As you were requiring the various ribbons for your men, we should take it as a compliment if you will allow us to offer the same without charge. Trusting this will be to your entire approval.
> We are, with respectful compliments,
> Your obedient servants, Pulford & Sons.

While it is true that the Gurkhas became known during the First World War, they still tended to be classified as one of India's warlike races, men with a martial reputation; they were bracketed with the Sikhs, the Garwhalis, the Dogras and other famous fighting men of the subcontinent. The fact that they came from Nepal, a country which was not part of the British 'Raj', was not generally known by friend or foe. But what was becoming famous—or notorious in German and Turkish circles—was their national weapon, the kukri, and it was about this time that the following oft-quoted story, garnished with many variations, made its rounds.

The Gurkha swung his kukri with a deft cutting sideways movement.
    'Ja! missed,' cried the German.

'Try shaking your head,' retorted the Gurkha.

There are more bloodthirsty versions of the above which, even if untrue, helped to inspire fear in the Germans' hearts.

Away from the Western Front when two Gurkha battalions were fighting guerrillas in Persia, after an encounter with them in mid-1918, we read about the Gurkhas 'getting well home into the enemy, which gave them a wholesome dread of the Gurkha kukri, the fame of which spread through the countryside!' The original Brigade, and its modern equivalent, Britain's Brigade of Gurkhas, has accepted, often with wry smiles, wild and exaggerated stories about kukris, knowing well that by so doing there are psychological advantages in encouraging an excellent propaganda weapon. The practice has continued to this day, including the Falklands campaign of 1982.

Soon after the Great War there occurred a horrifying incident about which the recent film *Gandhi* revived the controversy that raged over fifty years ago. In 1919 the Amritsar massacre took place and it is mentioned only because General Dyer pulled a party of Gurkha soldiers off a train and ordered them to fire on the crowd of some 5,000, gathered in the garden of Jallianwala Bagh. In the film—for reasons best known to the producers—Dyer, the British and the Gurkhas are all shown in the worst possible light. Without attempting to defend General Dyer, it must be stated that the majority of those who died (about 240) were not killed by the fire directed at them by the troops but died during the panic-stricken stampede to escape through two small exits. It is a pity when those whose task it is to entertain us present a biased version of an incident in history without acknowledging that there is another side to the story.

In June, 1921, the last Gurkha regiment returned to its peacetime cantonment from overseas, coming back from North-West Persia. Britain owed much to Maharajah Chandra Shamsher and as a mark of official gratitude, he was made a full General in the British Army, while to the nation of Nepal Britain made a gift of one million rupees, to be paid annually in perpetuity. Chandra Shamsher died in 1929 and was succeeded by his 60-year-old brother who had been Commander-in-Chief of the Royal Nepalese Army. Gradually the Rana regime was losing its hold over the country, although they were to cling to power until the early 1950s. The hereditary system of succession to the post of Prime Minister was shown up when Dim Shamsher survived his elder brother by only two years, to be followed by the fourth of the brothers, Judha Shamsher, who, although an old man and not in the best of health, continued as Maharajah until he voluntarily retired in 1945. The Ranas thrived on intrigue and nepotism was rife, so much so that by 1938 Judha's sons were installed in some of the most responsible positions in the country.

Judha was the last of the Rana Prime Ministers to exert absolute power in Nepal; he was a quick-tempered despot and inclined to be impulsive. On the other hand he was a hard worker and had regular contact with the string of applicants who petitioned him for his support or appealed against the decisions of his officials. This likeable man was a realist and was convinced that the British parliamentary system of democracy could not succeed in a country like Nepal, without anything approaching universal education or adequate communications. Nepal remained a backward, isolated kingdom under his rule and, as an illustration of that statement, there was no motor road connecting Kathmandu with India until the end of his days as Prime Minister. Indeed, it used to take 120 porters eight days to carry a motor car from the roadhead at Bimphedi over the hills into the Valley of Kathmandu. Within the Valley there were only some 400 cars and none of the roads penetrated up into the hills beyond the fertile plain which encircled the city itself.

Whatever defects Judha Shamsher might have had, he was a Gurkha and, having pledged his friendship, he did not hesitate when the Second World War started in 1939. At once he made a spontaneous offer of eight Nepalese battalions to assist in the internal defence of India, an offer that was eventually accepted. The so-called 'phoney war' during the winter of 1939 lulled the Allies into complacency. Permission for the Gurkha battalions in the Indian Army to go overseas was not sought until mid-1940 when the news from Europe was grim, with Great Britain left to fight on her own. At a time when it appeared as if Britain might be forced to give in, the British Minister went for an audience with Judha who was surrounded by Nepalese generals, several of whom doubted Britain's ability to stand up against the German onslaught. It was an historic occasion and when the Maharajah was asked for his permission to allow the Gurkha units to go overseas, he answered clearly, for all to hear, 'Yes. Of course.' Another question followed: Would he give permission for the Indian Army to increase its Gurkha battalions from twenty to thirty? Again looking only at the British Minister, the Maharajah repeated: 'Of course.'

The interview ended with words that have been recorded for posterity, words that serve as an example of how a true friend and a staunch ally felt about the British in their time of need:

'Do you,' demanded Judha, 'let your friend down in a time of need?'

'No, Sir, but there is often a difference between countries and individuals.'

'There should not be. If you win, we will win with you. If you lose, we will lose with you.'

The alacrity with which his sanction was given, when hopes of a victory were low, was heartwarming. But it was not to be the end: further requests from the British were to follow, first, for another ten battalions to form training centres and then, shortly afterwards, a special request for a battalion of 500 paratroopers to be raised. On each occasion the Maharajah did not hesitate and when, during the black days of September, 1940, London was burning from the blitz, there came another example of his generosity. When Judha learnt that the East End had been the target for the Luftwaffe, he ordered his Government to give the equivalent of 25,000 rupees in sterling to the Lord Mayor of London to be used to help the people in that distressed area.

During the Second World War the Gurkha Brigade was eventually expanded to forty-five battalions and ten training centres, nearly a quarter of a million of Nepal's manhood rallying to the cause of Great Britain. Once again their soldiers were to go to many parts of the world—to Iraq and Malaya, to Persia and the Middle East, to Cyprus, Italy and Greece, to Burma, as well as standing firm on the North-West Frontier and helping to maintain law and order in the cities of India.

Such a swift expansion, which saw the peacetime Gurkha Brigade more than double its size in a matter of months, inevitably placed an enormous strain on the small band of regular officers and senior Viceroy Commissioned Officers (Gurkha officers). To accentuate the problem, many of the staff-trained British officers were required to fill appointments at newly formed headquarters at a time when their experience was badly needed to raise and train the new battalions. To take their place, in ever-increasing numbers, came the wartime Emergency Commissioned Officers (ECOs), the majority of whom had never been east of Suez before and lacked any real experience of military life. After a concentrated six months' course at one of the

Officer Training Centres in India they were posted to a Gurkha training centre to meet for the first time raw recruits from Nepal who had never left their country before and certainly knew nothing about the white sahibs, now appointed to train them and lead them into battle.

When the ECOs reported for duty, proudly and self-consciously aware of the single black pip on each shoulder, they had their first meeting with the Gurkha officers, several of whom had been recalled from pension or whose retirement had been postponed so that they could play a vital role in transforming wild young hill boys, within the space of seven months, into soldiers.

The Gurkha officers, holders of the Viceroy's Commission, formed the connecting link between the senior NCOs and the British officers—as do their counterparts today in Britain's Brigade of Gurkhas. There are differences, of course, because the modern Queen's Gurkha Officers (QGOs) carry out their role in a different way, being better educated and more sophisticated than their forbears, though older generations of British officers maintain that they do not have the presence, dignity or bearing of their illustrious predecessors. Times change; suffice to say that if those who were at the hub of affairs during the Second World War could not cope with the pace of modern soldiering because of their lack of education, it is just as likely that the present-day Gurkha officer might lack the personality to have held sway over the constant stream of recruits that passed through the training centres between 1940 and 1945.

Armed with a smattering of Urdu learnt under a patient *munshi* (teacher) at the OTS, the ECO would find his few hesitant words barely sufficient to begin a faltering conversation with his senior Gurkha officer who, with infinite wisdom and a dry sense of humour, would correct grammar and vocabulary, and at the same time initiate the young sahib into the intricacies of the Gurkhali tongue. Every war-time officer can recall his own particular guide and mentor, the father-figure who welcomed him into the Regiment and the Gurkha Brigade as a whole. Subadar Hastaram Sunwar was the senior GO in 'E' Company at the 7th Gurkha Centre when the author joined. Straight as a ramrod, with his shirt and shorts starched in knife-edged creases, his chest ablaze with medal ribbons, Hastaram was putting on weight, but it only served to add to his dignified presence. On parade he treated his young officers as if they were gods, even when one of us made a mistake. When parade was over a dazzling smile would spread over his brown face as he would gently, tactfully correct our errors, always putting us at our ease even when we had perpetrated some heinous mistake or failed to act as '*sanu sahibs*' (junior officers) were expected so to do.

All the ECOs had their Hastarams and how much the Gurkha Brigade owed to them in each of the ten Training Centres which were filled to capacity for most of the war years. When the newly arrived recruits reached the Centre after the first train journey of their lives, the majority of them had never before seen a train, motor car, clock or even worn a pair of boots. They were like a cheerful shaggy crowd of half-grown puppies; they laughed when they should have stood silent, chattered freely in the ranks and spoke openly to the NCO about anything that interested them. For those first days they were all like our shepherd boy, Manbahadur Limbu, showing the basic qualities of the Gurkhas, their love of life, a natural warm sense of humour and an unconscious but fearless pride in their race.

In seven hard months those young boys became fully trained soldiers; it seemed impossible but the impossible was being achieved in each of the Training Centres. While they were changing, so, too, were the British officers as they learned Gurkhali, played games with the men and met the Gurkha officers socially after parade was over and gradually discovered more about the men they were aspiring to lead. The stocky, slant-eyed children of Nepal had now become trained recruits; their officers could see how they had changed from shy, unspoilt boys into seasoned riflemen, expert with their weapons and trained in many of the complexities of warfare that were to face them in the jungles of Burma, the deserts of North Africa, or in the mountains of Italy.

In the bitterness and shock of defeat, the glare of publicity did not shine favourably on the troops who fought in Malaya and Singapore or, a few weeks later, in the retreat from Burma. It was in the Middle East and Europe that the Gurkhas first gained publicity, thus causing an American editor in 1943 to say, 'Why have I not been told of these Gurkhas before?' More than anything else the award of the Victoria Cross to Subedar Lalbahadur Thapa in April, 1943, was to cause the Gurkhas to move into the limelight. He won his medal using pistol and kukri and the story hit the headlines.

Eventually the tide turned in South-East Asia and although he had—and still has—many critics, the man who played a big part in changing the state of affairs was Orde Wingate. He was attracted by the idea of British forces operating behind the Japanese forward position with all supplies and ammunition being airdropped whenever the situation so allowed. He was a man of restless temperament, eccentric in dress, speech and habit, whose personality has been described by many writers and whose exploits are still championed, disputed and denigrated by military historians. He only comes into this story because during 1943 a newly-raised Gurkha battalion went into Burma under his command. The unit had been selected because Wingate maintained that a newly-raised battalion could easily be moulded to his ideas: he accepted the inexperience of officers and men because he assumed responsibility for the training that, in his opinion, would outweigh their immaturity. It was a mistake because the unit was broken up, its sub-units intermingled with British soldiers and a large number of the Gurkha riflemen were employed as mule drivers. For the young men from Nepal, many aged only 16 or 17, the results were not fortunate. With hindsight we can say that if the battalion had fought under its own officers then the story might have been different; if the junior commanders had been more experienced and all the British officers fluent in Gurkhali, then the outcome might have been a happier one.

Although they had no previous experience as mule drivers, the Gurkha soldiers readily adapted to the task. One brigade Animal Transport Officer (ATO) has written, 'I was privileged to have elements from the 3/4th Gurkha Rifles [on the second Chindit operations], as mule-drivers and they were superb at all times.'

But even in the disaster of the first Chindit operation there were examples of the 3/2nd Gurkhas showing outstanding qualities of self-reliance in adversity. A *naik* and his section made their way back to India, existing for over three weeks on what they found in the jungle. Moreover, they had crossed the swift-flowing Chindwin, undeterred by the half-mile-wide river, using a bamboo raft which they had built and used at night. So much for the theory that Gurkhas can only soldier efficiently when their officers are there at their elbow to do the thinking for them.

It cannot be denied that there was considerable controversy about the first Wingate expedition. As I wrote in *Britain's Brigade of Gurkhas*:

Wingate was to criticize the Gurkhas as being mentally unsuited for the role given them during the first Chindit expedition. Events since 1948 have shown the Gurkhas to be ideal troops for guerrilla and anti-guerrilla warfare in the jungle. Their fitness, ability to carry great weights, and cheerful patience in discomfort and adversity have always existed. But, by splitting the men up, by mixing units and, quite simply, not understanding that Gurkha soldiers need a different type of leadership to the British, Wingate failed to exploit their basic qualities.

Let that be the end of the debate. As far as the Gurkhas were concerned, the first expedition proved nothing that was not known before and achieved little, while the lessons, if any, were mainly ones showing what must not be repeated.

Coinciding with Wingate's exploits, which attracted the attention of the Allied Press, 14th Army began to be recognized for what it was, an efficient fighting force under a great commander, General Bill Slim—himself an officer of the Gurkha Brigade. During the early defeats and disasters a low priority for planes, tanks and other weapons was given to the South-East Asian theatre and it was starved of the resources required to transform defence into all-out attack against the Japanese. It was during this period of want that the soldiers, with more than a little bitterness, christened themselves 'The Forgotten Army'. Later, after they had stood firm against the Japanese onslaughts on Imphal and Kohima, the men of 14th Army began to use the title 'The Forgotten Army' with pride, until it became one of praise rather than self-denigration. In 14th Army there were several Gurkha battalions, about one of which the commander of an artillery regiment wrote: 'I am just witnessing one of the most glorious sights of the war, the Gurkhas attacking'. While the world acknowledged that the Japanese was a brave fighter and a tough soldier, in Burma he met a man of equal courage and endurance. In addition the Gurkha had a natural skill as a tracker and could move through the jungles with a silence and patience that the Japanese could never match.

Another event which brought the Gurkhas on to the front pages of the English newspapers happened in early 1944, south of Rome, where the Allied armies were striving to break through stubborn German defenders who were helped by the inhospitable terrain and bitterly cold weather.

In March, 1944, three Gurkha battalions, serving in the then famous 4th Indian Division, were attempting to storm the German stronghold in and around the Abbey on Monte Cassino, a feature that guarded Highway Six, the main route to Rome. In the small hours of 16 March, the 1/9th Gurkha Rifles entered the rubble and collapsed buildings which were all that remained of the town of Cassino. The Battalion's task was to capture Point 435, an outcrop just below the monastery on which there was a shattered pylon which in happier days had carried an aerial ropeway. To the Allied soldiers this feature was known as Hangman's Hill and it was less than a hundred yards from the south-west corner of the monastery. C and D Companies of the 1/9th Gurkha Rifles were sent ahead to attack Hangman's Hill, with the rest of the Battalion following in single file. But C Company disappeared into the night and no one saw or heard of them until dawn was breaking, when German defenders in the abbey caught sight of the Gurkhas clambering up the rugged slopes below Hangman's Hill.

Under their young commander, 20-year-old Captain Michael Drinkall, the company had walked up a track in the darkness of a wet night and moved in single file diagonally across the hillside to a point where they had dumped their packs. This was below Hangman's Hill and in silence they crept up on the objective and surprised the German outpost in a small cave, killing two of the men they found there. Those who escaped raised the alarm which was followed by heavy mortar fire on to the Gurkhas crouching tensely behind rocks as dawn broke.

During this 'stonk' both the Company Commander and his Gurkha 2ic were wounded. Undoubtedly more casualties would have resulted had not Naik Amarbahadur Khattri, with great coolness, crawled forward and silenced the German mortar and its crew. The wounded Drinkall, who continued to command his men from a stretcher, had no communications with his Colonel as the Company radio set had failed. Two runners were sent off down the hillside towards an Allied outpost below Castle Hill, but they were spotted and nearly intercepted before returning from their abortive mission. C Company's position was not a happy one and Drinkall was on the point of arranging a withdrawal as soon as it was dark when, suddenly and dramatically, the Company wireless, after much tinkering, began to work and communications were re-established with Battalion Headquarters, situated on the edge of the town. Drinkall was told to hold on at all costs. That night the remainder of the Battalion began moving up the mountain while noisy diversions were arranged to cover their advance. Once again it proved quite impossible to move any other way than in single file and this slow and frustrating process

continued until dawn on 17 March. The first sub-unit reached C
Company's position at an opportune moment, because the Germans
had launched a sharp attack which threatened to overrun the whole
Company. The wounded Drinkall with a revolver in his hand had
inspired his men to hold on until the rest of their Battalion arrived.
The Germans were beaten off and retired to the monastery, taking
with them the news that a substantial force of Gurkha soldiers was
now within yards of the outer walls of the building. As soon as possible
the CO, Lieutenant-Colonel George Nangle, deployed his Battalion
into a tight little perimeter, ready for the next phase in the battle
which he expected would begin shortly afterwards. His Gurkhas had
taken their objective after moving up the mountain with little besides
their weapons and light scales of ammunition. No one had expected
this to be more than a temporary phase before the next move and
there had been no suggestion that these lightly-clad men would have
to endure a long sojourn on the rocky slopes of Monte Cassino. As an
officer was to comment: 'Now began our nine days' wonder!'

Inevitably during the difficult night advance up the steep rocky
slopes there had been some stragglers and some of these stragglers
had unusual adventures. Rifleman Manbahadur, lost in the ruins of
Cassino, took shelter in a wrecked tank. From this cover he shot a
German sergeant through the throat, dressed his victim's wound,
and eventually turned up on Hangman's Hill with a useful stock of
American cigarettes which he had found *en route*.

For nine days the ordeal of this Battalion continued, an ordeal that
made the 9th Gurkhas the best-known unit in Italy and, at that time,
in the United Kingdom as well. Clinging like limpets to their rocky
home in the shadow of the monastery walls, they were encircled by
tenacious German paratroopers from 1 Parachute Division, the *corps
d'élite* of the German army, who were well aware that the key to the
whole operation lay in Hangman's Hill. If the monastery was to be
stormed, then Hangman's Hill had to remain in the hands of the 1/9th
Gurkha Rifles.

As the hours passed, stocks of food, water and ammunition ran so
low that attempts were made to send in Indian troops, the majority
volunteers, who shouldered as many of the loads as they could carry
and guided by the Adjutant of the 1/9th, sallied out on to the hillside.
Unfortunately their presence was discovered and only a proportion
of them, after wandering over the steep slopes for most of the night,
found the Gurkhas at dawn, having narrowly escaped walking into

the monastery by mistake. They brought sufficient ammunition but very little food. Moreover, they arrived after daybreak—too late to return—and had to be allotted a defensive position on the northern slopes of the outcrop. By day and night the constant shelling meant that the number of wounded rose hour by hour and shelters had to be found, including a culvert under the road, and when this over-flowed, the wounded were placed in sangars along the embankment.

The senior Allied commanders appreciated that the supply line to the 1/9th Gurkhas had to be made safe, realizing that unless this was achieved no major assault could be launched from Hangman's Hill against the battered abbey. Not surprisingly the German paratroopers had other ideas and were determined to cut the jugular vein which passed through the precariously-held Castle Hill and other contested features on the mountainside. A series of attacks were pressed home with much vigour by the paratroopers against the key feature, Castle Hill, all of which were rebuffed but only with the greatest of difficulty. This meant, however, that plans to reinforce and supply the isolated band of Gurkhas were postponed. In the end re-supply by air was attempted and on the afternoon of 18 March, forty-eight aircraft, guided to their target by coloured smoke, made their first drop on Hangman's Hill. The release of the parachuted supplies was accurate but, because of the steep hillside, many of the canisters bounced out of reach of the garrison. Less than half were recovered and once again little food was forthcoming. The choice of rations for the battalion, the majority of whom were high caste members of the Chettri clan, was not imaginative, but hunger and necessity overcame religious scruples. Officers and men tightened their belts and made do by sharing packets of American 'K' rations. Communications, too, suffered when all the radio batteries dropped were either lost or smashed: moreover a number of men were wounded by German snipers when they rushed out in gallant but forlorn attempts to retrieve the precious canisters.

A few of the canisters contained rum and one officer was to write, 'One biffin [Gurkha rifleman] got hold of a jar of rum and as darkness fell Gurkha music was heard across the hill'. It was a typical example of Gurkha aplomb, the ability to make the best out of a situation fraught with danger.

Days passed, while below Hangman's Hill the battle gradually developed into a stalemate. The Germans' aggressive countermeas-ures had spelt the end of any attack on the monastery, although

Colonel Nangle's force had received reinforcements in the shape of two rifle companies from the 1/4th Essex. They were companies in name only because barely seventy men from the two companies eventually reached Hangman's Hill and many of them had been wounded in encounters with Germans during their hazardous ascent from Castle Hill. At top level a decision was made: the 1/9th Gurkha Rifles would have to abandon Hangman's Hill, a decision not understood by many of the Gurkhas who immediately asked which unit was to relieve them. On 25 March the withdrawal began after dark, with the tired force moving down the route used by messengers despatched earlier that day. Various distractions were made by other units with artillery concentrations being fired against certain German outposts in the town, while New Zealand tanks displayed aggression in as noisy manner as possible. The withdrawal down the hillside was a considerable strain on men who had endured so much for so many days but it passed without any major incident. In fact, the Germans appeared to have had scanty information about the Gurkhas on Hangman's Hill, chiefly because they had decided to let them wither away rather than attempt to remove them by force in a series of direct confrontations—which would have been bitterly contested and therefore costly in lives. Certain it is that the Gurkhas' withdrawal from Hangman's Hill was not reported to higher headquarters until twenty-four hours after it had been completed.

Down from Hangman's Hill Colonel Nangle led a party of eight officers and 177 soldiers from his own battalion, supported by two officers and fifty soldiers from the Essex Regiment and forty Indian soldiers from the Rajputana Rifles. Later, German patrols claimed to have counted 185 dead Gurkhas in and around the craggy feature—the price the battalion paid for the nine days spent under the shadow of the abbey. From Nangle came warm-hearted praise for the support given by the gunners, 'we loved them after Hangman's Hill', the signallers and porters, and finally, for the incredible courage, patience and fortitude shown by the wounded as they lay in the open awaiting evacuation, or in many cases, death. 'Comparatively little could be done for them. Yet there was never a word of complaint, never a suspicion of self-pity nor any indication that things were anything but normal.' For Nangle and his 1/9th Gurkhas came messages of congratulation from many quarters. The Corps Commander, General Sir Bernard Freyberg, VC, was to write: 'What I particularly liked was at no time was there any belly-aching from 9 GR'. Although the

Allies had failed, once again, to take Monte Cassino, the Gurkhas had won themselves high praise for their ordeal on Hangman's Hill. On the crest of that shaggy outcrop a giant boulder today bears the 9th Gurkhas' badge, 'The story of how men won and held that eyrie in mid-air will be told again and again as long as memory remains'—in such a way does their Regimental History end the account about this action.

With the European war drawing to its end, inevitably the spotlight switched to South-East Asia where the Japanese, although very much on the defensive, were fighting for every yard against odds that entertained no chance of final victory. Being opposed by such a stubborn foe in dense jungle or thick scrub, it is not surprising that bouts of close-quarter fighting were far more common than in the Middle East and European theatres. At close quarters individual acts of courage and leadership were far more noticeable: seven Gurkha soldiers were to win the VC during the Burma campaign, as against three in Africa and Italy. They were:

Burma

Havildar Gaje Ghale	5	GR
Rifleman Ganju Lama	7	GR
Rifleman Tulbahadur Pun	6	GR
Subedar Netrabahadur Thapa	5	GR
Naik Agamsing Rai	5	GR
Rifleman Bhanbhagta Gurung	2	GR
Rifleman Lachhiman Gurung	8	GR

Italy and Africa

Subedar Lalbahadur Thapa	2	GR
Rifleman Sherbahadur Thapa	9	GR
Rifleman Thaman Gurung	5	GR

It will be noticed that six of the recipients were riflemen, a remarkable fact because opportunities for conspicuous individual acts of gallantry and leadership rarely present themselves to junior ranks. One of the riflemen, Ganju Lama, had won the MM about a week before he was awarded the VC for supreme valour. Even more remarkable is that in peacetime Ganju Lama would not have been recruited by the Gurkha Brigade: indeed, he slipped through the net by enlisting under an assumed name and, moreover, was a citizen of Sikkim. He was also wanted by the police—albeit for a comparatively minor misdemeanour.

One of the Riflemen, Tulbahadur Pun, continued serving with the 6th Gurkhas until he reached the rank of Warrant Officer, being given honorary rank of Lieutenant (QGO) before going on pension. Many years later, on 10 December, 1980, Tulbahadur visited the British Gurkha Centre at Pokhara to meet the Prince of Wales. It had taken him some twelve days to make a journey which normally took him four days; he had recently been knocked off a cliff by a boulder and had been unconscious for two days. On regaining consciousness he started coughing blood but he gradually got better. At Pokhara, after meeting Prince Charles, he was advised to go to hospital where an examination showed that the old man had broken one shoulder and smashed six ribs. The doctors were amazed when they heard that he had been walking over mountain tracks for twelve days with such injuries. Tulbahadur had not lost the qualities that had won him a VC over thirty-six years before.

The Second World War ended in the late summer of 1945 and within a few months the battalions raised during the war years were disbanded. Scores of veterans were sent back to civilian life, the majority of whom were not entitled to draw any sort of pension unless they were disabled, and even then they received a sum that we in the Western world would consider paltry.

Even for those selected to serve on in the twenty regular battalions the future was bleak, as an unsettled subcontinent groped its way to Partition. No one knew whether the Gurkha Brigade would continue as a single entity and if it did so, in which army it would serve— India's or Great Britain's. The months of uncertainty were made worse by a spate of rumours.

In the event, four Regiments were earmarked to serve HMG, two from West Nepal (2nd and 6th Gurkha Rifles), and two from the East (7th and 10th Gurkha rifles). Thereafter followed a period of confusion leading up to the 'opt', as already mentioned in Chapter 3. It was a direct result of so many deciding to remain in India that the hectic spate of recruiting had to be carried out early in 1948 in order to bring the four Regiments up to strength.

Away from battle and just to show that Gurkha sentries were as alert then as those doing duty today—and as predictable in their rigid compliance with orders received from above—two stories are recounted from a Second World War veteran's 'memory bank'.

A Gurkha battalion was stationed in Iraq and the officers were in their mess, having a drink before dinner, when the Gurkha orderly officer came to report to the CO: 'Sahib, we have arrested an officer sahib and we have got him in the guard tent.' The Colonel told the Gurkha orderly officer to bring the 'prisoner' to the Mess, together with the sentry who had arrested him. They both duly arrived and all present were surprised to see that the officer under arrest was the Brigade Major. He was full of apologies. It appeared that his identity card photograph, when taken originally, had shown him with a moustache, which he had since shaved off, and as the photograph did not show his present likeness, he had been arrested by the sentry. The CO called forward the Gurkha sentry, gave him a packet of cigarettes and complimented him on his efficiency. The Brigade Major was rewarded with a drink!

Later in the war, the CO of another Gurkha battalion detailed a rifleman to guard the approach to his Battalion Headquarters, with strict instructions that no one was to pass that point. He then went off in his car to visit another unit, little knowing that his Divisional Commander was going to pay his unit a surprise visit. The Gurkha sentry saw the General's staff car approaching and ordered its Sikh driver to stop, which he did. The Divisional Commander and ADC were sitting in the back. Angrily the ADC instructed the driver to drive on. The Sikh obeyed the command and the staff car moved off, whereupon the Gurkha sentry raised his rifle and put a bullet in each of the back tyres. At the time the General was furious but later, when the CO returned to his headquarters, the senior officer had cooled down, even to the extent of complimenting him on the efficiency of his sentry as well as expressing admiration of his snap-shooting!

Such tales may make us smile and certainly every officer who has ever served with Gurkhas can produce his own favourite yarn about sentries. Nevertheless, when we analyse the stories, one fact will emerge every time: the Gurkha sentry may have appeared to be inflexible but he was complying with the orders as he understood them. '*Jo Hukum*' ('Whatever the order') was the motto of the famous 4th Indian Division. It was one that was honoured and obeyed by the Gurkha Brigade wherever its members served between the years of 1939 and 1945.

Twenty-one years later when a Gurkha battalion was about to leave Borneo and was having one or two rather hectic farewell parties, a newly arrived rifleman went on guard for the first time. His NCO questioned him carefully to make sure that he knew all the right procedures and the correct passwords. Finally the NCO said:

'Right, *keta* (lad); you are on duty and it is about one o'clock in the morning. You see a figure crawling through the grass towards you. What do you do?'

Without hesitation, the young sentry replied: 'Help him back to the Officers' Mess.'

Such an appreciation of the situation, following his recent arrival, says much for the Rifleman's intelligence, and for his sense of humour.

SIX

True to their Salt

Although the popular image of the Gurkhas may be that of short stocky warriors, wielding their wicked kukris in a bloodthirty manner, they have won an equally high reputation in other aspects of soldiering. When engaged in keeping the peace, a job which requires a deep and genuine understanding of the civilian population, their tolerance, patience and lively sense of humour have proved invaluable assets; these qualities have made them excellent ambassadors, not only for their own country but for the British Army. Perhaps their most delightful gift is the immediate bond they seem to have with children, irrespective of colour, creed or race, a trust inspired by their uncomplicated attitude towards life and their smiling faces which encourage confidence and affection.

No one would dispute that the most demoralizing thing that can happen to a soldier occurs when he is forced to surrender to an enemy in battle, before being marched away to a prisoner-of-war camp. It is an experience that is impossible for anyone to conjure up who has not suffered such a fate.

Like their British comrades in arms, many members of the Gurkha Brigade had to suffer long periods of captivity in both World Wars. In Mesopotamia a whole battalion was taken after Kut-al-Amara fell in April, 1916; some twenty-five years later, the same battalion was led off into prisoner-of-war camps when Tobruk surrendered. A few months later three Gurkha battalions from different regiments disembarked at Port Swettenham in Malaya, only to take part in the demoralizing retreat back to Singapore, which surrendered in February, 1942, with the survivors being herded into improvised cages and camps by the Japanese. From the accounts studied, there appears little to choose between the Turks and the Japanese as captors, neither exhibiting much respect for their prisoners, conditions being usually inhumane.

Back in 1915, by their discipline and behaviour in captivity after the fall of Kut, the men from the 7th Gurkhas were to win the reluctant admiration of their Turkish guards. When the British and Gurkha officers were separated from the men, the senior NCOs took control of the junior ranks and throughout the protracted months under appalling conditions they rarely allowed discipline to falter.

This was a remarkable achievement, especially after Kut, one of the most abject capitulations in British military history. There followed a terrible march northwards through the desiccated provinces of the Turkish Empire into pestilential prison camps. Here they lay half-starved and ill-used until, in the last months of the war, they were released. How was it, then, that the 7th Gurkha NCOs held their men together through such a horrifying ordeal?

In his last address to the battalion in Kut, they had heard their Commanding Officer stress the need to uphold the Regiment's name, and nobly did they obey his orders. As a direct result of this cohesion and *esprit de corps*, the Battalion suffered far fewer casualties as prisoners in Turkey than did other units held under similar conditions. Their conduct was not without reward for it won the grudging but genuine respect of the Turks and Germans; it also won the healthy regard of the Arabs, so that the treatment to which they were subjected, deplorable though it often was, never reached the callousness of that handed out to the disorganized, the abject and the stragglers. When forced to march from one camp to another there was no straggling; each Gurkha soldier took strength from his comrades: cohesion and membership of the *paltan* was never forgotten. Three senior Non-Commissioned Officers took over command, ran the battalion and carried it triumphantly through every trial so that when it disembarked in Egypt after Armistice Day, it bore itself as smartly as it had done in 1914 when it first set foot in Suez. One survivor was to report that standing orders were observed,

At the sound of a whistle, orderly Non-Commissioned Officers doubled to receive their orders. On falling in, section commanders called their rolls, and a word of disapproval was the severest punishment ever resorted to or required.

History was to be repeated during the bitter days of February, 1942, when the British surrendered Singapore to the Japanese. For the Gurkhas who were marched into captivity it was to be a grim long-drawn-out struggle for survival, a supreme test of loyalty to their regiments and allegiance to the British. Like the Turks before them, the Japanese quickly separated the Gurkhas from their British officers, but at the beginning treatment was lenient, in an attempt to persuade them into joining the newly raised Indian National Army (INA). Few, very few, Gurkhas were to join and several of those who did did so only to try to escape from Japanese forward positions in Burma at a later stage in the war. Apart from one or two 'line boys', the rest were unmoved by Japanese promises or threats. Inevitably the junior ranks looked to their Gurkha officers for guidance, and the Japanese realized that it was necessary to break the resistance of those leaders.

As an example of leadership by a Gurkha officer, a party of some forty young soldiers, just out of recruit training, joined the 2/1st Gurkhas in Malaya and were taken prisoner. Under Jemedar Jasbahadur Rana, IDSM, they were incarcerated in Penang gaol. Apart from the Jemedar, the soldiers' knowledge of Hindi or Urdu was rudimentary. In gaol they were visited by Captain Mohan Singh who had been in touch with the Japanese before hostilities had begun and had immediately defected to them, whereupon his new-found friends promoted him 'General' in charge of the INA. Mohan Singh harangued the Gurkha party in fluent Urdu about the advantages of joining the INA and promised that anyone who wanted to leave gaol with him would be a free man. He ended his talk with the command, *Uthao* (Get up). This was the only word one young Gurkha recruit had understood in the whole talk and his instant reflex at being so bidden by an officer was to leap to attention. He was the only one; with a bellow, Jemedar Jasbahadur Rana shouted, *Bas!* (Sit down), which the unfortunate lad did with even greater alacrity. And that was that—a nil haul!

After the war ended 'General' Mohan Singh was tried for treason in the Red Fort in New Delhi and found guilty. But when India received its independence he was pardoned—much to the disgust of thousands of loyal Indian army officers and men.

The Gurkha officers were rounded up and taken to concentration camps where they suffered every indignity, being forced to work at demeaning tasks while their guards beat them with bamboos or clubbed them with rifle butts. They were deprived of blankets; no shelter was allowed at night or protection from the heat of the sun by day; the little food they were given was so disgusting that starving animals would have been reluctant to eat it. The senior Gurkha officers suffered the worst hardships. Subedar-Major Harising Borha, blind, demented and suffering internal haemorrhages, died after severe beatings and other ill-treatment. This gallant officer refused to submit to the Japanese demands and addressed a letter of protest, pointing out that his countrymen were not citizens of India and therefore were not interested in serving in the Indian National Army. They had taken an oath to serve the British King-Emperor and as prisoners-of-war they were entitled to honourable treatment under International law. This letter, couched though it was in the most dignified manner, caused the series of brutal beatings which killed him. Inspired by their Subedar-Major's unflinching courage, his men stood firm and it was on their testimony that this great Gurkha officer was posthumously awarded the Indian Order of Merit (IOM) when the Japanese surrendered.

After their failure to win over the Gurkha officers, the Japanese turned their attention to the NCOs, separating them for intensive indoctrination which included lectures that went on into the small hours of the morning. The NCOs held out, even refusing to sign for their pay in case they should unwittingly enrol in the INA.

At the same time leaflets, couched in the following terms, were circulated to all the camps which contained Gurkha soldiers.

Dear Gurkha soldiers!
One cannot describe the condition of the Gurkhas who were sent to fight in the Far East.
The Britishers left us, the Gurkhas, to meet a living death, to face hardships and fight against odds in the jungle of Sittaung and Moulmein, when they withdrew themselves. The whole of the youth of our land have been snatched from our land. Who are to defend our sacred Nepal from the Chinese aggression from the North?
The British have fully exploited us. Why fight for them who want to keep you slaves? Why not join hands with those who are to destroy and wipe them totally thus bringing happiness to all.

Your Gurkha Brothers.
Indian National Army

The leaflets were used by the prisoners for a variety of purposes! Having failed by lectures and the written word, the Japanese tried various tactics, ranging from sheer brutality to bribery by offering luxuries, and even appealing to the Gurkhas to side with them because of a distinct similarity in physical appearances. While all this was going on, let us not forget that their British officers were suffering intense hardships and brutal treatment, many being sent to work as coolies on the notorious railway line that ran from Siam into Burma, the 'Railway of Death'. Before they were separated by too many miles a handful of officers risked death or, at the best, severe beatings by making secret visits to see their beloved Gurkhas who had served them so well.

Those unfortunate British officers who had been detailed to work on the infamous railway never saw any of their men until the end of the war. On the railway, first under Major Paddy Sykes of the RASC—until he was killed by an Allied air raid on the POW camp— and then under 'David' Davidson of the 4th Gurkha Rifles, a 'communication system' was established. In Davidson's words:

> Basically this consisted of notes on our life and conditions being hidden in certain specified prearranged places by a British lorry driver who drove the Jap NCOs into the nearest Siamese town each week. These were picked up by the house servant of a Briton, married to a Siamese, who was in an internment camp in the same town and allowed his wireless and comparative freedom. He in turn sent us the main headlines of what was happening in the world. The wife, who was not interned, was pally with the wife of the French Consul at Saigon, who used to pass our news to the outside world by diplomatic means. The curious fact was that, in our eyes, the servant stood out as being unusual in the extreme: he was Chinese, wore a white solar topee, had a large prominent wart on his face and dressed in semi-European clothes. Yet to Asian and Jap eyes, he could not have aroused suspicion since he was never questioned, let alone picked up!

The modest 'David' Davidson makes no mention of the dangers involved in acting as organizer of the 'communication system'. It needs little imagination to realize what his fate would have been if the Japanese had realized how the leaks to and from the outer world were being organized under their very noses.

As far as the junior Gurkha POWs were concerned the Japanese did not use kid gloves for long. In the words of one young soldier who spent four years as a Japanese prisoner,

> A sick man sent to the hospital never returned recovered. Due to the scarcity of medicines in the hospitals no sick man survived during our days in prison. Sometimes the Japs would ask us to join their army and on negative answer, they would treat us more severely. They even opened fire on our camp ... No one at that time hoped of being able to return safe to his homeland.

The writer, then a rifleman, was to end his distinguished service as Honorary Lieutenant Aitasing Gurung, MC—and his recollections close with these words: 'Having read this, you will be able to imagine what it was like to be a prisoner'. In peacetime it is not easy to do so—but fortunately the passing years soften memories of pain and mindless cruelty.

The various regimental histories pay tributes to the bearing of the men when they formed up once more as a battalion after their ordeal was over. One account was to describe how

> The ragged troops left the train and amongst the noise and confusion our small party quietly fell in its sections and half-companies, reported to the Commanding Officer and marched away. Little was said at the time but that evening many spoke with praise of what they'd seen—an example never to be forgotten.

Those men had come out of Turkish prison camps: years later, another unit, after surviving Japanese cruelty and ill-treatment, was described by their CO, himself a prisoner, as being

> Indeed a wonderful sight, all scrupulously clean and neatly dressed in ancient and patched clothes, sometimes in garments made by themselves ... Having had lunch with the Gurkha officers—my best meal in $3\frac{1}{2}$ years—I held a parade to give the men a *shabash* (well done). To my amazement they marched as smartly as on a peacetime ceremonial ... Their soldierly behaviour and appearance brought tributes from everyone!

So, in spite of the inevitable feelings of demoralization after being taken prisoner, the evidence is that the vast majority of Gurkhas kept faith and that their self-discipline did not disintegrate during the black years of captivity.

We must not forget that it is the duty of every officer or soldier, after being taken by the enemy, to attempt to escape, should such an opportunity occur. Such escapes required great initiative and daring—coupled with self-reliance—and most important of all, good fortune. In the First World War prison camps in the centre of Turkey presented a truly formidable prospect for a successful escape and not surprisingly there were to be very few. One party under Padamdhoj Limbu of the 7th Gurkha Rifles escaped from the Taurus Mountains in 1918 and was picked up by the Australian Light Horse in Aleppo— a magnificent achievement under any circumstances. In the Second World War there were so many gallant escapes and evasions of capture that it is difficult to know which to describe and which to leave out. Away from the forward areas escape from the Japanese was nigh on impossible. Nearer the front line, opportunities did occur, such as when Subedar Nardhoj Rai, with other men from his battalion, was captured in February, 1942, near the Sittang River. After a terrible time in several camps, where they suffered illness, torture and in-human degradations, the men survived to work on the 'Railway of Death' in Siam. One day, under cover of a torrential rainstorm, Nardhoj and two of his men escaped and made their way north to cross the high mountains into China where, at first, they were taken for Japanese and viewed with great suspicion. Fortunately, by using the few words of Burmese which they had learnt, the Gurkhas were given help and passed from village to village, right across north Burma until men of a Kachin tribe guided them to the British forces on the Indian border. Subedar Nardhoj Rai estimated that they had covered over 1,500 miles.

Rifleman Gangabahadur Gurung of the same regiment had the misfortune to be captured on two occasions by the Japanese—only to escape twice—a gallant feat which cannot have been accomplished by many in any theatre of the War, let alone in the Far East. On both occasions he escaped during Allied bombing raids and, not surprisingly, his nickname in the regiment thereafter was 'Japan'!

Escaping from Japanese camps in the rear areas verged on the impossible but evading capture after operational setbacks or am-bushes was easier because the friendly Burmese hill tribes had an effective resistance organization and these brave folk helped British,

Indian and Gurkhas who were hiding from the Japanese. Another unusual story concerns Bugler Randhoj Rai who, after being captured in early 1942, worked as a coolie under the Japanese on road and rail construction for over two years. One day, when the Chinese Army attacked the labour camp, he escaped with two other Gurkhas and they eventually joined the United States Forces in North Burma. Randhoj ended his story by saying:

> I was put into Company X of Baluan Wagon Force. I was with them for two months when we laid ambushes and killed Japanese. I carried the Bren gun. Knowing that the British forces were near I was granted permission to rejoin them. During all this time I kept my bugle. The Japanese could not blow it so they let me keep it. It now hangs in the Officers' Mess of our First Battalion—with my name on it.

Buglers seem to claim their fair share of adventures in these pages. The last story from the Far East concerns Lance Naik Narbahadur Thapa of the 1st Gurkhas. He was a prisoner for about a month in Malaya until he met another Gurkha who lived near his village in Nepal. Without telling us how they escaped, the records show that the two men eventually joined up with Chinese guerrillas living in the jungle nearby, before going with them on raids against the Japanese. Thereafter they lived with the Chinese in the jungle and had to attend Communist indoctrination sessions, as well as officially enlisting as soldiers in the Malayan People's Anti-Japanese Army (MPAJA).

The Japanese eventually reacted to the pin-pricks administered by the guerrillas and, apart from carrying out air raids, sent strong punitive forces into villages in the area. But as the Chinese had already warned the local inhabitants, the majority of the people had taken shelter in the surrounding jungle. Thereafter conditions for the guerrillas improved and just before the war ended, in June, 1945, much-needed ammunition, food, arms and clothing were dropped by parachute, the planes coming over at night. They also dropped a wireless set and it was on this radio that the two Gurkhas heard that the war was over when the Japanese surrendered on 14 August, 1945. By that time everybody in the camp was armed, even the women, and in Narbahadur's words, 'When we heard of the peace there was tremendous rejoicing'. Little did he realize that these comrades of his would be using those same weapons against British and Gurkha soldiers in less than three years' time.

Escaping from the Germans and Italians was considerably easier and for the 7th Gurkhas the habit started as soon as Tobruk fell. One NCO, Havildar Singbahadur Rai, managed to get out of Tobruk and set off across the desert towards Egypt. His greatest enemy was lack of water but, fortunately for him, he met some friendly Arabs who helped him to survive. With astonishing hardiness, he walked across over 300 miles of the hostile and almost waterless desert that separated Tobruk from Alamein. Later, four other men of the same battalion completed the journey, a wonderful example of fortitude and resolution. Others were not so fortunate when, after remaining at large for several weeks and suffering terrible hardships, their ordeal was rewarded by captivity.

After being held in temporary camps in North Africa, the majority of the Gurkhas were then sent to more permanent prisoner-of-war camps in Italy. Once again it was only to be a question of time before several escaped. In most cases the escaped Gurkhas reported that the Italian people were friendly, although they had to be on their guard against the diehard Fascists who seemed to be present even in remote mountain villages.

Havildar Harkabahadur Rai, after being captured in Tobruk, escaped, only to be recaptured a few hours later. He was in an Italian prisoner-of-war camp for the next fifteen months before an opprtunity arose for him to escape again. For three months Harkabahadur hid in the mountains, only to be found by the Germans and sent to Epinal in the South of France. A few days later the Royal Air Force bombed the camp and in the confusion Harkabahadur escaped. After wandering about the countryside, he joined up with a party of Maquis led by an American colonel. In Harkabahadur's words:

> We did a lot of marching, occasionally going in MT. We laid ambushes and attached German posts along the border of Switzerland. We destroyed all the telegraph wires and electric cables for miles around. I think that it was some time in August, 1944, that the Germans attacked our camp. I had the job of holding a road block and shot about twelve magazines into the advancing enemy. My party also knocked out a German tank. Eventually the Germans retired and we continued to use the camp as a base for operations.

Harkabahadur was unduly modest when telling the tale of that action and it was only later that he admitted that he had to take command: 'the rest were quite useless'. He was with the Free French for over five months and received the Military Medal as well as medals for gallantry from the French and the Americans. After the war was over, Harkabahadur, by now a portly gentleman, became Mess Havildar of the Officers' Mess, where he presided over the mess orderlies, and the young sahibs, with genial, avuncular firmness. One day, when Harkabahadur was not wearing his impressive medal ribbons, an officer from a British unit nearby jokingly claimed that Gurkhas were wooden-headed, lacked initiative, and required detailed orders before they could carry out the most simple of tasks. When he was told that the Mess Havildar had commanded a party of Maquis in France—which resulted in him receiving three decorations for leadership and courage—the visitor's face was a study. After hearing a couple of stories from Harkabahadur, he left the Mess declaring that he would never again question the Gurkhas' ability to think and act on their own.

The urge to escape, the desire to fight on, was to be demonstrated over and over again. The following short tale is not a POW story but admirably illustrates that urge. The Burma Army had retreated in 1942 but during the months that followed many stragglers were still crossing the border into India. It must be borne in mind that the vast majority were stragglers through no fault of their own; when units were cut off, individuals and little groups of men had to try and find their way back to India as best they could. One day a British officer from a Gurkha battalion was leading a patrol back into Burma when along the jungle track came a lone Gurkha. He was naked but for a ragged pair of shorts and a battered Gurkha felt hat; he was near starvation and his feet were bleeding. On his shoulder he carried an LMG. The British officer said, 'Come, let me carry your Bren gun.'

The soldier replied, 'Sahib, I have carried this gun since well before the Sittang battle. I will carry it until I find my regiment.' He was escorted to the end of his lengthy ordeal by the officer and his patrol, all of whom understood why the soldier was determined to complete his own mission unaided.

It is stories like these that prove the point that was made when we started with the shepherd boy, Manbahadur Limbu, way up in the Himalayan pastures, grazing his father's flock. Illiterate and uneducated, certainly, but from an early age that boy had learnt to stand on his own feet, to make decisions—albeit in familiar surroundings—and to use his common sense to solve problems in a practical way.

Perhaps the most amazing evasion of all ended on 29 October, 1949, when a Gurkha patrol from 1/10 GR, pushing their way through deep jungle in Malaya, came upon a small shack. Thinking that it had been built by the Chinese Communist Terrorists, they surrounded it, their weapons at the ready. Inside there was a solitary man who the patrol thought was Chinese. On closer scrutiny and interrogation he was identified as being a Gurkha and, to their surprise, he named Major Charles Wylie as one of the officers he had served under in the 2/1st Gurkha Rifles during the War. Charles Wylie had been Adjutant of that battalion and, by a strange coincidence, was now serving in 1/10th Gurkha rifles during the Malayan Emergency.

For the first time in seven years the unkempt Gurkha began speaking in his own language and the story he had to tell was an extraordinary one. His name was Nakam Gurung, a naik of the 2/1st Gurkhas who, during the long retreat in Malaya in the first few weeks of 1942, had contracted a bad bout of malaria. So bad was he that his Subedar had left him in the jungle with a supply of rations and some medicine, with instructions to await the return of the British Army. Unfortunately Major Wylie, the Subedar and those who survived the retreat went into prisoner-of-war camps until 1945. Nakam recovered from his illness but, alas, there was no sign of the British or Commonwealth troops.

It appears that he contacted some Chinese on the edge of the jungle who helped him to set up his hideaway. Naturally they were afraid of being caught helping an Allied soldier by the Japanese, so they told him not to contact them again. Thereafter for seven years he had lived on his own, existing on wild pig, fish caught in traps and a variety of jungle fruit. He had no idea the war was over. During that long vigil, Nakam saw and heard men dressed in jungle green on more than one occasion. Thinking that they were Japanese, he remained hidden, but it now seems evident that they were Chinese Communist Terrorists or, just possibly, a friendly Gurkha patrol.

Mentally, Nakam was surprisingly stable and, after a few days in normal surroundings, he was sent back to the 1st Gurkha Centre, which by now was part of the Indian Army, where after some understandable red tape shown by an unbelieving Pay Office, he drew seven years' back pay and went on leave to Nepal. Warning was sent

up to his village just in case his appearance caused him to be treated
as an evil spirit, belatedly returning home from the war. It is nice to
recount that the Indian Army promoted him havildar until he had
completed his fifteen years' service to earn a full pension when he
retired.

Being a countryman and used to fending for himself, Nakam was
able to survive. More surprising perhaps was the fact that his sanity
was unimpaired by being an involuntary hermit for over seven years.

In complete contrast to escapes and evasions, but very much in the
'True to their Salt' tradition, is the story of Chakkemba, about
whom three articles appeared a few years ago in the 10th Gurkhas'
Regimental Magazine. For Chakkemba—or more accurately Chokemba—did not want to go anywhere, not even home: his aim was to
stay put looking after the battalion garden and he did just that—for
much of his 45 years in the Regiment.

His full name was Chokemba Limbu and he hailed from the village
of Majhuwa near the River Maiwakhola in the heart of the Limbu
clan country. Not that he saw very much of his village after enlisting
in 1901 because he was still serving at the end of the Second World
War. Chokemba became an institution in the 1/10th Gurkha Rifles
and, once he had established his claim to be the battalion gardener,
no one could move him, though several attempts were made to send
him on pension at various times in his service. On one such occasion,
having been given an uncompromising '*pinsion jan-na*' (I won't go on
pension), his Company Commander decided to try a new approach
and went to visit the old warrior in his garden. In the late Brigadier
Michael Roberts' words,

> Chokemba was reclining on a charpoy, under a shady tree, from
> which a network of strings stretched away to various fruit trees and
> vines. The other ends of the strings were attached to suspended
> kerosene oil tins containing a few pebbles so that all that was needed
> to scare away marauding birds was to give the proper string a jerk,
> thus setting up a hideous jangle in the required area. He produced
> his regimental mufti 'pillbox' from somewhere, rose sedately and
> having saluted, asked me what I'd come for—but he knew!

The then Major Roberts told him that he had come to look at his
garden and the old boy said, provided that was the true reason and
nothing else, he was welcome, otherwise he wasn't!

Presently I asked him why he didn't want to go on pension, to which he replied that the Government could stop paying him as a rifleman if they liked but he wouldn't take a pension and he wouldn't go. It was some time before he finally came out with what, I believe, was his real reason and it was this. His father, and I think another close relative, had gone on pension and hadn't lived long enough to draw the first instalment and he knew that the same thing would happen to him if he accepted a pension.

Perhaps that explains everything but the episode took place in 1927 and Chokemba was to continue serving for another twenty years. By that time his thrift was a byword; he never parted with money unless he was compelled. Going on one of his infrequent furloughs, he travelled with several other soldiers by train from the North-West Frontier to Darjeeling. When he arrived at the recruiting depot near the town, he was most upset to find he had spent four annas on the way. He went about shaking his head and muttering, 'How did I get rid of all that money?'

Just before the Second World War began, it was decided that Chokemba really must go on pension. He was duly despatched with some others but, when the truck got back from the station, the old man was still in it. 'I cannot go on pension. What would the battalion do without me? And they say there's a war coming.' He was allowed to stay.

Some years before this his wife and daughter had come to take him home. They were able to get in to see the CO before meeting Chokemba, and the wife pleaded that the old man be sent home with her. The Colonel agreed and off went the two women to find their tame warrior. But Chokemba had heard and was furious; so angry was he that for a whole day he locked them up in a hut in his garden and only released them when they agreed to go back quietly to Nepal without him.

Lieutenant-Colonel H. C. S. Gregory tells another story which throws more light on this remarkable old Gurkha soldier. It was told him by Honorary Captain Dalbahadur Limbu, IOM, MC, who revered the old Rifleman.

It happened at Quetta when Chokemba's wife and daughter were living with him in the family lines. Whether or not Chokemba had warning of what was afoot is by no means clear. But if he did, he gave no sign of it in the way he handled the situation.

In accordance with custom the suitor, no longer very young but in every respect it seems most eligible—for was not a 7th Gurkha Rifles Quartermaster Havildar, in peacetime at that, a man of some standing?—arrived at Chokemba's quarter accompanied by three or four grave-visaged Gurkhas of his own *jat* (clan), smartly attired in regimental mufti and bearing the usual gifts of fruit, chickens and rum. Seated outside the quarter they began to talk of this and that, not looking particularly at Chokemba's door, as if their destination was still some way off.

After a while Chokemba emerged, greeted them casually and sat down to join in the desultory talk. He would have noticed the deferential manner of the visitors and the fact that their gifts were placed close to his door. He appeared to be pleased as if appreciating that all this was doubtless their way of doing honour to his age and well-known length of service.

'Sooner or later a man marries,' said one of the vistitors, as if informing the company of something that had recently come to his notice.

'They are fortunate who have parents to arrange everything for them,' said the 7th Gurkha Quartermaster Havildar. He fixed his gaze on a distant object and continued, 'But in a strange country the custom cannot always be observed.'

Chokemba frowned and it was clear that further hints were becoming unnecessary. 'It is true that men marry,' he said, 'some in the hills and some in the lines, but a man who has only one daughter and is growing old would not willingly let her go to another man's house.'

He rose with the grimaces and noises appropriate to age and long service and moved the Quartermaster Havildar's gifts from just outside to just inside his door.

'You have observed the customs very creditably,' he remarked, 'and showed great respect to this poor and stupid man. But it seems somebody is seeking a wife and if I had two daughters gladly would I give him the more beautiful of the two. You have brought all these gifts and come a long way. I cannot disappoint you. I will do my best. Quartermaster *guruji*, I cannot give you my daughter but you will not go back empty-handed: you can take my wife.'

What happened next was not clearly related. By all accounts the

Quartermaster Havildar of the 7th did not accept Chokemba's offer nor it seems did he wait to see if any of the customary gifts could be recovered.

Having been allowed to stay on during the Second World War, Chokemba did the jobs of *mandir* (temple) orderly and hospital orderly. Aged though he was, he was a useful member of the unit at a time when experience was at a premium. The war ended; it was decided that the time had at long last come and Chokemba absolutely must go. Now, reluctantly, he agreed to do so but it seems he made good terms for at his last final parade he was given a large gold medal and invested with the local rank of Havildar.

Sadly, he survived only for a few years and in 1951 the news reached the 1/10th Gurkhas that Chokemba had died peacefully in his home. As Colonel Gregory said, 'No doubt when the time came he was as reluctant as ever and made the best terms he could.'

A future recruit?

A man from the hills

Machhapuchare from Pokhara, West Nepal

Three generations

An old-age pensioner

A typical village street in Nepal

Say your prayers first

Porters of Nepal

The Pied Piper and his recruits

Traditional dance, West Nepal

Six brave men – Gurkha VCs of the Second World War

Maruni

General Sir Walter Walker, KGB, CBE, DSO; the Brigade's most distinguished officer in post-war years

Queen's Gurkha Orderly Officers of 1954 in full regalia

A study in concentration — a piper of the 6th Gurkhas

On river patrol in Brunei

The Gurkha Paras receive their Red Berets

Above: Crossing a river in Borneo

Right: H.H. The Sultan of Brunei presents a cheque for the Gurkha Welfare Appeal in 1968 to General A.G. Patterson, CB, DSO, OBE, MC

On guard near the Indonesian border during the Confrontation

'The best-dressed men of the year' — men from 1/7th Gurkha Rifles going on leave to Nepal after the Falklands Campaign

Above left: Ready for anything — 1/7th Gurkha Rifles in the Falklands

Left: Showing the strain — 1/7th Gurkha Rifles in the Falklands

A temple in Kathmandu

SEVEN

War in Peace

In early 1948 Britain's newly acquired regiments left India for Malaya with a variety of emotions, ranging from nostalgia for the past, sadness at handing over well-ordered and established regimental depots to new guardians in the shape of Indian officers, and relief at getting away from an increasingly difficult situation. Without taking sides, it must be admitted that there were a few ill-natured wrangles over what was to be handed over to the Indian Army and what was to be taken to Malaya.

The frenetic period of recruiting, described in an earlier chapter, which began in January, 1948, was instrumental in bringing the four regiments, each of two battalions, up to strength—on paper at least—but there were many shortages. Undoubtedly the most serious was the dearth of senior Gurkha VCOs (retitled King's Gurkha Officers in the British Army), so that the first few months were a considerable strain on the handful of British officers present. This was aggravated by the fact that the strange and sometimes complex form of British Army administration had to be learnt from scratch by young, inexperienced Gurkha clerks. The early days in Malaya would have been difficult enough even under peaceful conditions; time was needed to settle down; but this precious commodity was not to be granted because, with dramatic suddenness, the Communist insurrection broke out.

Within days the Security Forces and the Government were fighting hard to prevent Chin Peng and the Communist bandits—soon to be called Communist Terrorists (CTs)—from overrunning the country. The infantry units were so hard-pressed that even the recruits were sent out to guard vital points, and on certain occasions into the jungle, without even having fired their weapons on a range. Not surprisingly, they were ordered to use their kukris and bayonets in an emergency, rather than risk hitting their friends firing live rounds for the first time. As our American friends succinctly put it: 'They were training for real.'

The Gurkha battalions were learning their trade as jungle fighters against an enemy who had received their initial training from British instructors and liaison officers during the war. The Chinese terrorists were masters of the jungle and they lived in its depths, coming out from time to time to commit atrocities. The onslaught of murder and arson terrified most of the local inhabitants who, without the guarantee of adequate protection, were reluctant to give information to the Government's forces. Witnesses to atrocities would plead ignorance rather than face the wrath of the Communists. To counter this dearth of operational intelligence the Security Forces had to go into the jungle and search for the Terrorists. Not surprisingly, there were several setbacks during the initial stages of the Emergency. As one company commander was to put it, 'I remember that we put more reliance on rifle butts and kukris at this time than bullets!'

If the first few months of the Emergency were hectic and at times frustrating, nevertheless the tempo of operations meant that in a remarkably short time the 'new look' battalions became more effective and increasingly efficient. Living and operating under jungle conditions enhanced the comradeship between the British officers and their soldiers, the jungle being no respecter of persons or rank. Major or rifleman, captain (KGO) or lance corporal, five days' rations and all the necessary ammunition and kit had to be carried in a large pack by each member of the patrol. Living cheek by jowl, often for weeks on end, there might have been a tendency to forgo discipline with undue familiarity between ranks but, surprisingly, this was not to be. Or, perhaps, not surprisingly to those who know the Gurkhas well; they have an innate ability to adapt to circumstances with a readiness that we, in the Western world, cannot match. A QGO can go to the United Kingdom on a tour and be fêted, even presented to The Queen at Buckingham Palace, and then, barely a few weeks later, be back in the semi-primitive conditions of his mountain village in Nepal without batting an eyelid. So shared discomforts in Malaya did not change the relationship between officers and other ranks; instead the trials that beset them all had the opposite effect, because the most junior rifleman could see that his British commander was a man like himself, capable of withstanding the physical challenges that faced them both, as well as shouldering other responsibilities while leading the patrol.

The sheer professionalism of the Gurkha soldiers enabled them to learn their trade as jungle fighters in a remarkably short time and, as the eight battalions, serving in Britain's Brigade of Gurkhas, were to continue to operate in Malaya throughout the Emergency, with the occasional break in Hong Kong, this was bad news for the Communist Terrorists. Not only did the Gurkhas learn to move through the dense forests in silence but their natural countryman's sense enabled them to meet the jungle on even terms, instead of viewing it with suspicion as an enemy—like so many British National Servicemen, hailing as they did from big cities. Carrying five or more days' rations as well as ammunition and other necessities in big unwieldy packs might have constituted a heavy load for the average European: for the highlanders from Nepal, well used to carrying even heavier loads in equally difficult terrain, such burdens did not pose any problems.

In the early days of the Brigade, there was a definite inclination on the part of the War Office to treat the Gurkhas as if they were African colonial troops who, unlike the Indian Army, had an establishment containing British warrant officers and NCOs as well as officers. A most dangerous misconception was that a permanent cadre of British officers was deemed unnecessary, a view that was supported by the CIGS (Field-Marshal Montgomery). It was known that he advocated that all the officers should be seconded and at that time there were other senior generals in the British Army who agreed with him. Such a concept struck at the very heart of the regimental system and, if it had been implemented for any length of time, the close family spirit of the Brigade would have been damaged beyond repair. The average Gurkha rifleman will follow—to death if necessary—any officer in whom he has faith, and faith only grows as a result of mutual trust through shared experiences. After that it becomes a matter of honour for the Gurkha to obey the orders of *Hamro Sahib* (our officer), in whatever task he may be ordered to perform.

Fortunately for the Brigade, Field-Marshal Montgomery's successor as CIGS was none other than Field-Marshal Slim, so that thereafter nothing more was heard about running the Brigade with seconded officers. One regiment in particular awaited the new CIGS's decision about their status with bated breath. A few weeks before the first shots of the Malayan Emergency were fired the two battalions of the 7th Gurkhas were told that they were to become Gunners as a first step towards the formation of an all-Gurkha Division which would eventually contain its own supporting arms and services. The news had been greeted with dismay, especially by the older British and Gurkha officers. No one, however, ducked the challenge, but the worsening state of the Emergency meant that the task of switching from their infantry role was one of considerable magnitude. Nevertheless, the 7th Gurkhas did adopt their new titles of 101st and 102nd Field Regiment, Royal Artillery (7th Gurkha Rifles) as a visible sign of their future role. Two ex-Indian Army Mountain Gunners were selected to command the two Battalions and with them came other gunner officers on secondment. Companies became batteries and the first forty officers and men moved to a nearby field regiment Royal Artillery to carry out a six-week course in gunnery.

Three signallers were sent for intensive training with the Royal Signals but at that time their knowledge of English was scanty, nor did their British instructors understand Gurkhali. Consequently, communication in the classroom was established by speaking Italian when it was found that the older members of both races had served in Italy during the War. A start had been made, but in the middle of June, 1948, the Malayan Government said it did not want embryo gunners but trained infantry, so any further steps in the conversion training were terminated for the time being.

In 1949 Field-Marshal Slim decided that the 7th Gurkhas would change back from being gunners to their traditional role as infantrymen. Batteries became companies and bombadiers became corporals overnight. And, once more, their own permanent cadre officers returned to the fold.

Gradually, over the next twenty years or so, the standard of living of the Gurkha officers and men, of the wives and children living in the unit lines, were improved until it could no longer be said that the Gurkha Regiments and Corps were the poor relations of the British Army.

Searching for Terrorists was something that the stocky men from Nepal tackled with quiet efficiency and it was not long before the Brigade had eliminated more than a quarter of the total number of the CTs accounted for by the Security Forces—although the number of Gurkhas fighting at that time was a very long way below a quarter of the total number of troops deployed. Once more the Gurkhas' reputation became highly coloured, many picturing them as savage little men who delighted in killing. Inevitably, in any race there are cruel men but the average Gurkha soldier looks upon killing in much the same way as his British counterpart, as a painful necessity that must be carried out in accordance with orders. Where duty must be done then there is no hesitation, but once the action is over they are a gentle race. The following short stories about an elephant and a tiger cub illustrate the point.

A patrol, on an abortive mission as far as CTs were concerned, was moving in single file along a jungle track when it came upon a baby elephant caught in a trap. The trap was a hole about eight feet deep and eight feet square, with vertical sides. It had been dug by aborigines who had to protect themselves and their meagre crops against wild pigs, elephants and other game. The trap had been dug on a track which was known to be used by wild elephants and, after the digging had been completed, the hole had been covered over with bamboo, earth and leaves.

The young elephant was very thirsty and very frightened. If the Gurkhas had been heartless they might have left it to die or shot it. The corporal in command of the patrol decided otherwise: he put out sentries to guard against the CTs and sent two riflemen in search of the aborigines' clearing to borrow implements with which his men could dig. When they returned, the patrol set to work to construct a sloping ramp. The digging was not easy and by the time they completed the ramp they were hot and thirsty. The corporal gave his men permission to drink from their water bottles but at the sight of water the baby elephant came trumpeting, unhurt, from the pit. He soon learnt to take a water bottle from the good-natured Gurkhas and pour the contents into his mouth. Getting the animal out had proved easier than they anticipated but getting rid of him thereafter proved impossible. Jumbo was determined that he would never be thirsty again so he followed the patrol, thundering this way and that, uprooting saplings and eating the leaves. Any chance of contacting the ever-alert CTs had been lost for ever. He drank at streams whenever the Gurkhas refilled their water bottles; when he was thirsty on the march, he felt for a soldier's water bottle with his trunk, whereupon the obliging Gurkha watered the elephant rather than himself. For two days he followed the patrol to its rendezvous on a main road where transport was waiting for the men. The elephant needed little coaxing before scrambling into a three-tonner, backed up against a bank with a bucket of water in it, to begin his journey to the unit lines, his new home.

At Battalion HQ Jumbo became a great favourite and wandered at will round the tents and 'bashas'. Indeed, the Gurkha Major had on one occasion to shoo him away when he tried to follow a defaulter in front of the Commanding Officer. Unfortunately, he grew apace and so did his appetite, so that food became a problem; he uprooted the young banana trees in the Mess garden and also uprooted a flagpole. He had outstayed his welcome. The Sultan of Perak saved the situation when he decided to claim Jumbo as royal property, although the gesture was not appreciated by the battalion when it was later learnt that the Sultan had sold the elephant to a circus for several thousand dollars.

The other visitor came to the sister battalion of the same Regiment—a six-week-old tiger cub with a snub nose. A lance-corporal and five riflemen had gone out to ambush a track along which it was thought that CTs might move. The soldiers were in position just after dark because they expected their enemy to appear later in the night when the moon was out. They had not been in position long when there was the roar of a tiger near their position and, thereafter, throughout the night the crashing of the animal and even its breathing could be heard as it prowled around the silent Gurkhas, hour after hour, emitting a series of roars which not only kept them alert but effectively frightened off any bandits. As morning approached the lance-corporal appreciated that the enemy would not come and stood up, signalling to his men to do likewise. The tiger also heard the signal, for there was a loud roar and two of the men saw the back and tail of a tiger as it bounded away through the scrub where the ambush was laid.

Under the direction of the lance-corporal the men, more from curiosity than for any other reason, searched the area and found traces of two tigers, one of whom they supposed to be a tigress because, deep in the grass, they saw a miserable, cowering tiger cub. They reckoned it had been deserted and decided to carry it back in a haversack to their camp where they fed it from a bottle. It was about the size of a large cat.

They named her Nepti which is Gurkhali for 'snub nose'. In Nepal Gurkha children—and some adults too—are given nicknames in accordance with their looks or physique. Thus snub-nosed individuals invariably are called Nepti.

The tigress settled down to life in a Gurkha battalion and became a great favourite with everyone. But as Nepti grew bigger and bigger so did her appetite. She remained tame and playful, although, unfortunately, she did not always know her own strength. There was never an instance of her actually hurting anyone, but it was clearly only a matter of time. In those days the rations issued to a Gurkha battalion consisted of goats on the hoof, so that goats frisking about the camp were not an unusual sight, while chickens were sometimes kept near the cookhouses and ran about unpenned. Nepti often made passes at the goats and chickens and on one occasion she was even seen stalking a Gurkha baby in the family lines. This led to her being kept on a lead until the decision was made to send her to a zoo. After negotiations had been completed Nepti was flown to London Zoo where she, in turn, gave birth to cubs, and thereafter was visited by many Gurkha soldiers when they were on duty or attending military courses in England. She remained an honorary and much loved member of the Regiment and retained her Nepali name until her death in 1958.

For the vast majority of the officers and men who served during the Emergency in Malaya, it was surprising how little wild game they encountered when on operations, although often finding the footprints of elephants or witnessing the ravages of wild boars. Perhaps their eyes, ears and senses were tuned in to seeking signs of the other inhabitants of the jungle, the CTs, whom most Gurkhas preferred to call 'bandits' despite officialdom decreeing otherwise.

Looking back from some thirty years, veterans who served in Malaya seem able to recall a surprising number of experiences in the jungle including, possibly, encounters with the CTs, even though the majority of contacts were over in a few minutes or even seconds. That they do so is natural because on operations each individual had his own particular part to play, irrespective of rank, age or service. This was in contrast to most of the major battles of the Second World War when participants felt powerless to act, feeling like tiny cogs in a machine and having little say in their destiny.

Before we leave the infantry regiments in Malaya it is well worth telling a story about a very tall officer—about 6′7″—who joined the 2nd Gurkha Rifles. It was not surprising that the Quartermaster had no jungle boots to fit his shoe size of 14.

Eventually a solution was reached; the officer would wear size 12s, the largest available jungle boots in the QM's stores, with the toes cut out and two pairs of grey worsted socks to keep out the thorns while, in the meantime, a special order for ten pairs of size 14 boots was sent to the factory, who promised delivery within a few months.

It transpired that the officer had to face a busy period of jungle operations which meant going through many size 12s and worsted socks as well as suffering badly-stubbed toes. Finally, on returning from an operation and with a few days' leave to spend in Singapore, he was overjoyed to hear that his new, specially prepared, jungle boots had arrived and his orderly was told to collect them from the QM.

Leave over and preparing for the jungle once more, the tall Sahib discovered, to his horror, that his faithful Gurkha orderly had carefully cut out the toes from all ten pairs of the new boots. So it was back to the size 12s, the worsted socks and stubbed toes.

It is right and fitting that the operational exploits of the Infantry battalions have been given pride of place—for two important reasons. Firstly, the Brigade grew from an untried mixture of wartime veterans and recruits into eight efficient battalions, highly skilled in jungle operations. The operational records of the battalions from 1948 until the end of the Emergency are remarkably similar; the names differ, locations alter, but the mode of operating, the successes obtained, and the routine that became a veritable way of life, followed much the same pattern in each of the battalions. Secondly, if the Brigade had not been on the ground during the dark days of 1948 and 1949, there is little doubt that Chin Peng and his MRLA would have won the day for Communism in Malaya.

The Infantry having been applauded, it is time to pay tribute to the two specialist Corps which were formed during the early days of the Emergency. The original idea had been to raise a complete Gurkha Division, one that contained the normal mixture of arms and services, but, at a time when infantry manpower was at a premium, the early concept was modified until only two Corps were raised in 1948. Although affiliated to their parent Corps in the British Army, these units were, and still are, an integral part of the Brigade and are so designated in the Army List. The reasoning behind this apparent anomaly was to ensure that all Gurkha soldiers, irrespective of arm or service, were administered by the same Gurkha Record Office in the Far East.

The Gurkha Engineers and Signals were formed in 1948—or to be more accurate, steps were taken to raise the first squadron of each of these Corps towards the end of that year. The first major task carried out by the Gurkha Engineers was the construction of a new road between Gemas and Rompin which included a 342-foot timber-piled bridge, soon to be known as Gurkha Bridge. That bridge, completed by two of the field squadrons during 1955, was to herald a multitude of other tasks such as building roads, constructing airfields and helicopter landing-zones all over Malaya, culminating in a joint venture in the State of Kedah with British and Malayan engineers on a project which was to last three years. More often than not their work was designed to open up communications to enable the Security Forces to have quick access when mounting operations against the CTs. By the end of the Emergency the Gurkha Engineers had earned themselves the reputation of being thoroughly efficient, with specialists who could operate all the same plant and machinery as their British counterparts. As we will see later, their role in the Borneo Confrontation was to be of paramount importance.

Likewise the birth of the Gurkha Signals began towards the end of 1948 with a small cadre of Royal Signals officers and a few unit signallers from Infantry battalions acting as a training team. During the months that followed the cadre instructors trained up the necessary tradesmen to form the first Independent Brigade Signal Squadron so that, by the end of 1950, Gurkha Signal personnel were able to provide the communications for a brigade on active service in Malaya. From this modest start, and as more and more tradesmen were trained, Signal troops were deployed to the other formation headquarters and by 1954 the Signal Regiment was manning all the communications at the operational headquarters of 17 Gurkha Division. Initially, all officers and men in the Regiment wore the Royal Signals cap badge but in 1954 a new badge incorporating the Royal Signals badge and crossed kukris was approved: in such a way the infant Regiment retained its links with both parents.

Towards the end of the Emergency detachments from the Regiment were sent to Nepal to provide much-needed communications for the first-ever democratic election held there.

A third Corps was raised in July, 1958, under the title the Gurkha Army Service Corps, later in 1965 to be redesignated the Gurkha Transport Regiment. Being formed at the end of the Emergency meant that the fledgling Corps did not see active service in Malaya, but during 1959 two companies were pronounced ready for operations anywhere in the world, with one company moving to Hong Kong while the other remained in Malaya. Shortly afterwards two other

companies were raised, thus completing the Regiment's full establishment. It cannot be denied that there were several critical and diehard
British officers in the Brigade who were horrified when they learnt
that a specialized Transport Regiment was being formed, their main
criticism being that Gurkhas were not natural drivers, having to learn
their skills by rote rather than with any natural inspiration. There
was an element of truth in this allegation. Their background was
against them being natural drivers but what they lacked in experience
was compensated in full measure by their keenness to learn. As a
consequence, the most junior Corps in the Brigade, the GTR, quickly
established an enviable reputation.

When peace returned to Malaya the Brigade proudly exhibited
mementoes of the Emergency such as captured weapons, terrorist
uniforms, headgear and other trinkets. Perhaps one of the most
amusing was a label from a bandit medicine bottle. It is quoted here,
using its original spelling and grammar.

TAKE ON TONG (famous for chi Kit Pills).
This wonderful pills has been very effective in curing the following
diseases as;—
Headache, Fever, Cough, Indigestion, Nauseating, Vomiting, In-
creased Salivation, Foul Copper—Breathing, Furred-Tongue,
Gumboils, Continuous Spitting, Mistiness, Tiredness, Dizziness,
Sea-sickness, Stomach-ache, Constipation, Rheumatism, Tooth-
ache, Insect Bites, Ect.
Directions; take Half-bottle for adult, twenty pills for children, ten
pills for babies' with warm water.
(Pregnant women Can Be Taken).

Perhaps the secret weapon which cured all ills but lost the war!

Before we leave Malaya, let us look at the final report to the King
of Nepal. In 1959, and in subsequent years, the Major General
Brigade of Gurkhas went to Kathmandu where, in a special audience
with HM The King, he presented his annual report on Britain's
Brigade of Gurkhas. That year he was to say:

I am happy to inform Your Majesty that consequent to the unrelent-
ing efforts of the troops, the successes which they have achieved
against the Terrorists of Malaya have resulted in all except one
battalion (near the Thailand Border) being withdrawn from oper-

ations. The Brigade has earned a further 43 rewards for gallantry in the field and the total now gained by Your Majesty's subjects is 443.

Let those words summarize the part played by the whole Brigade of Gurkhas in saving Malaya from the Communist threat. As a result that multi-racial country survived violence and bloodshed to enjoy a peaceful start as an independent nation. It is pleasant to be able to record that its people did not forget their Gurkha friends when, as we shall see later, the Brigade was forced to make hundreds of serving soldiers redundant, many of them without a pension. At that sad time, the citizens of Malaya and Singapore gave generously to the Gurkha Welfare Appeal. The Brigade's part in the struggle against Chin Peng's CTs was remembered with gratitude by people from all walks of life—Chinese, Malay and Tamil, as well as Europeans.

Apart from the successes on operations, prodigious strides had been made in a vast range of activities. Gurkha boys were selected to go to Sandhurst as officer cadets and became the forerunners of the RMA-trained commissioned officers, now found in every battalion. Children's schools were set up and further education made possible for the more intelligent children living in the family lines. Married quarters for the families, with appropriate medical and welfare facilities, changed from the primitive into something akin to the standard found in the equivalent British units nearby. And, by no means the least significant concession, Whitehall agreed to carry out a regular review of the Gurkha soldier's pay and allowances to keep these in line with inflation. By 1960 it really could be claimed that the Brigade had become part of the British Army.

There were, of course, certain aspects of life in the British Army which the Gurkhas found difficult, especially when selected to be Mess waiters in an officers' mess. One amusing menu was recorded by an officer who, after being given 'scream blood eggs' for breakfast, said it was no surprise, later that day, to be faced with a dinner consisting of:

Clear Soap
Fried Seoul
Rust Beef
Yak Shirt Pudding
Mushed Potato

Kabaj
Prun On Toast

If that was indeed a faithful record of a menu in 1959, it is fair to say that most modern Gurkha Mess Waiters would have the menus typed and spelt in near-perfect English. Nevertheless, even in 1982 there was to be an amusing misunderstanding of the English language, entirely true but with no names mentioned for obvious reasons.

Early that year in the New Territories of Hong Kong a major Gurkha Field Force social event had been planned and, as is usual on these occasions, orderlies to assist in the serving of drinks were drawn from all units. To co-ordinate the event, a rehearsal was held the preceding afternoon and orderlies were detailed to their particular tasks. One party had been detailed to hold silver trays with a variety of drinks at the entrance and were carefully briefed on exactly what they were carrying. This being a major function attended by the 'top layer' of the Hong Kong Government, the major drink featured was 'Buck's Fizz'. A suitably strong Gurkha was nominated to hold the tray and was briefed on the content of the glasses.

The function began and a few minutes later a very senior lady alighted from her car and advanced to the silver tray of 'Buck's Fizz'. 'Is that orange juice?' she enquired. To which she received the unblinking reply: 'No ma'am, it's Ox Piss.'

She drank it!

New ground was broken in 1962 when, for the first time ever, some 1,700 Gurkhas were stationed in the UK. Accompanying HQ 63 Gurkha Infantry Brigade (retitled 51 Brigade in England), went the 1/6th Gurkha Rifles, 68 Gurkha Field Squadron, 247 Gurkha Signals Squadron, and 30 Squadron of the Gurkha Army Service Corps. In addition, a small proportion of the married men were accompanied by their wives and children, the whole contingent being accommodated in Tidworth.

One lighthearted incident in which the author played a minor part happened during that first autumn at Tidworth. With trees around the parade ground busily shedding their leaves, one Saturday morning men of the Brigade Defence Platoon were told to sweep up the area. A week later the author (then DAA QMG) turned up at his office to see at least a dozen Gurkhas up various trees, shaking the branches vigorously with a Gurkha sergeant urging them on to greater things.

'Sergeant, what the hell are they doing?'

'Sahib: the *keta* (lads) are getting fed up with this Saturday "fatigue" so we thought we'd finish it, once and for all today.'

Wisely, the author decided to stay in his office until the deed was completed!

As part of the strategic reserve the Gurkha contingent trained in England and Wales, Denmark, Germany and Aden, as well as surviving a bitterly cold winter exercise in the then peaceful Northern Ireland. At the time the intention was to grant each of the eight battalions a tour in the UK with a similar roster for the other squadrons from the Gurkha Engineers, Signals and Service Corps Regiments. Events were to rule otherwise, for which President Sukarno of Indonesia was largely to blame.

After the Malayan Emergency was over there was an interlude with no operations apart from the occasional battalion on active service near the Thailand border where Chin Peng and his followers enjoyed comparatively safe sanctuary. For those in peacetime stations it was a return to 'spit and polish', to courses of instruction and cadres, to training to improve their ability to move anywhere, on light and airportable scales, at the drop of a hat. It was as well that officers and men of the Brigade had prepared themselves because in December, 1962, someone in Headquarters Far East dropped his hat without warning. Within a matter of hours two rifle companies from the 1/2nd Gurkha Rifles were on their way to the small State of Brunei, to begin the first of several tours that were to be spent by each of the Brigade's battalions and squadrons from the Corps in the Borneo Territories.

The short interlude was over. Now, with hindsight, it is clear that if that interlude had gone on for a further three or four years, then the rundown of the Brigade would have started earlier and it would have been an extremely truncated formation which emerged at the end—or, even more likely, it would have seen the demise of the Brigade as part of the British Army.

After the Brunei rebellion had been quelled—in which the determination shown by the first two companies that landed played no small part—the spark of revolt flared up across the border in Sabah and Sarawak. The man responsible for this was the flamboyant dictator, President Sukarno of Indonesia, who was trying to satisfy his dreams of grandeur. Sukarno saw himself as the head of a large confederation of states—a Pan-Indonesia which was to include Malaya, Singapore and the British colonial possessions of North Borneo. Also included in his dream was the tiny oil-rich State of Brunei and this was one of the major reasons for the revolt. After it had been put down, the Sultan of Brunei made it quite clear that he did not want to participate in any future Federation of Malaysia but wished to continue as a British Protectorate. This status endured until the end of 1983 when, a trifle unwillingly, the Sultan accepted independence.

Britain's participation in the Confrontation in Borneo was played down for mainly political reasons. The final victory which came in 1966 was not even celebrated because so little was known about it in the outside world. It began in 1963 when a raid was launched against the police station of Tebedu in Sarawak; thereafter Indonesia strove to unsettle the border tribes while establishing her own military bases along the long frontier dividing Kalimantan [Indonesian Borneo] from the British colonies. And what a border it was. Borneo is the third largest island in the world and the frontier stretches from end to end, along nearly 1,000 miles of mountain, river, swamp and tropical forest. To defend that frontier called for skill, courage and the intelligent application of the troops available. 'Dominate the jungle' was the directive given to his Forces by the Director of Operations, Major-General Walter Walker, himself an officer of the Brigade of Gurkhas with many years of jungle fighting behind him, first against the Japanese in Burma and thereafter against the Terrorists in Malaya.

In the surveillance of the Kalimantan border the SAS took a leading role, acting as the eyes and ears of the Security Forces along the ill-defined frontier. There were never enough of them, however, and the newly-raised Gurkha Independent Parachute Company was ordered to help the SAS in their formidable task. There had been Gurkha paratroopers during the Second World War when 153 and 154 Battalions had been formed from volunteers to become part of the 50th Indian Parachute Brigade.

One Second War veteran recalled how initially volunteers were sought from the one unit which had been selected to be converted into the first Gurkha Parachute battalion—provided sufficient men volunteered. The problem was how to put the idea over to the 750 men of the 3/7th Gurkha Rifles in a hurry.

Explanations were not effective so a film was shown, but there had been no time to run it through first. The film began with the words: 'Now if you do your job well, there is no reason why 95% of these men should ever reach the ground alive.' It was a film designed to teach ground troops how to deal with a parachute attack! It was a great success because all the Gurkhas saw was parachutists raining down from the sky and rolling about on the ground. There was plenty of fighting and they thought it tremendous fun! The whole battalion volunteered!

However, age and a series of strict medical inspections reduced the number considerably, so volunteers were sought from other Gurkha battalions.

A British officer was taking a party of volunteers by train to join 3/7th GR from another unit to start their training as future parachutists. Indian trains were apt to stop in the middle of nowhere, for no apparent reason, and this is just what this train did. It happened that the train had stopped by an aerodrome, so the officer thought he would take the opportunity of showing his men what an aeroplane looked like.

He got them out of the train and took them across the airfield, where they saw an aircraft parked on the runway. They then saw the pilot walk across to the aircraft, get into it, taxi down the runway and take off. The officer turned to the men and said 'Now don't you think that was marvellous?' One of the Gurkhas replied, 'We don't think that was marvellous. The Sahib gave the order for it to fly, so it must fly.' It would not happen today. Nepal is now air-minded!

The original paratroopers trained hard for three years, patiently waiting for an opportunity to be used as parachutists on active service. When the chance came, they were dropped near Rangoon where they encountered a fanatical group of Japanese who had either been left behind to observe or had been forgotten by their superiors when the order to abandon the city had been given. It was unfortunate that the majority of the Gurkha casualties that ensued were caused by American aircraft which hit the paratroopers harder than the Japanese did: an ill-aimed stick of bombs tragically brought death and under-standable bitterness at the time.

Now there were Gurkha paratroops once more but, after carrying out their training in the early 1960s, it was to be as surveillance troops, operating on the ground in small parties, that the Gurkha Parachute Company was initially to be used in the Borneo campaign.

Prior to that Rifleman Dikbahadur Chhetri was to get himself in the Brigade's annals for an extraordinary feat of toughness, even by Gurkha standards. He was participating in an exercise jump which took place over Sabah, some six hours flight from the RAF airfield at Changi on Singapore Island. During the flight Dikbahadur was airsick. When it was his turn to jump, his canopy did not develop properly but the Rifleman was in such a turmoil that he failed to pull his reserve parachute. Not unnaturally, Dikbahadur landed badly, was unconscious for forty minutes and only remembers waking up in Jesselton hospital some fifteen hours later. Miraculously, he was able to rejoin his unit in time to fly back with them to Singapore. After reaching Singapore, Dikbahadur was sitting in a vehicle when another military vehicle ahead ran off the road, injuring twelve men. With others, he dashed to the rescue and helped to get them into the nearest civilian hospital. Following all this excitement and exertion, he fainted and was admitted to the same hospital—for the wrong reasons! Only later was it found that he had broken his back in three places. Dikbahadur complained only when he learnt that he could not jump again with his Company during the following week! Of such men was the Gurkha Parachute Company composed and it was sad that during its short existence there was never an opportunity to jump 'in anger'.

Apart from their surveillance duties, the Gurkha paratroopers had another unusual role to play during the Confrontation. Before they could take up their SAS-type assignment, all ranks had to undergo a concentrated bout of specialized training, which included medical courses, signalling, survival techniques, river crossing and many other facets of the multifarious tasks which 22 SAS take in their stride. Thus equipped, members of the Company were selected to train local Iban and other Borneo tribesmen who were being enlisted into an organization called the Border Scouts.

Some of the paratroopers led an extremely lonely existence when they were sent out to be in charge of a group of Border Scouts, who were tasked to act as 'eyes and ears' astride likely incursion routes from Indonesia. It was not an easy duty for a young lance-corporal or senior rifleman to perform because it required tact, tolerance, initiative and a high degree of self-discipline. Temptations there were as the majority of Dyak longhouses contained a friendly and hospitable people, never tardy with generous potions of their home-brewed liquor, often dispensed by comely bare-breasted maidens who were neither shy nor aloof. It would be a brave man—or a naive one—who claimed that every Gurkha soldier during his detachment duty acted like a puritan of old. It would have been out of character if they had behaved like monks, since the average Gurkha likes his *raksi* (spirits), gambling and women. That there were liaisons there can be no doubt but rarely—if ever—at the expense of their high military standards or to the detriment of their operational duties.

Surveillance continued to be all-important, even when Sukarno escalated the level of conflict from minor raids by 'volunteers' to incursions by the TNI (Indonesian Army). By this time every Gurkha battalion was serving a series of six-month tours in the Borneo Territories. The Gurkha infantrymen were quick to learn how to dominate the jungle and thus to own the frontier. The ambush became the key operation both for the guerrillas and the Security Forces. An ambush required all the tricks of the Gurkhas' trade: an eye for country, camouflage, silence, fire control, guile and, above all, self-discipline. There was no chance of ambushing the enemy if the Gurkha smoked, chewed gum, washed his hands with scented soap, cleaned his teeth, Brylcreamed his hair, whispered or coughed at the wrong moment. In ambush, the Gurkha lay in wait for the dangerous Indonesian raider whose sense of smell and keen eyesight were truly remarkable.

Subsequently General Walker, the Director of Operations, wrote:

The Gurkhas were able to live in the jungle as close to the animal as was humanly possible to do so, and became so well trained that they were able to fight the guerrillas both in the jungle and out of it, and to kill and harry them until they were utterly exhausted. . . . The type of fighting, the type of country and the climate call for individual stamina and fortitude, stout legs, stout hearts, fertile brains, and the acceptance of battlefield conditions almost unimaginable in their demands on human endurance.

It is not necessary to enlarge on this graphic description by someone who knew far more about the conditions than any other senior officer in the British Army at that time. But while the Gurkhas were outfighting the Indonesians at their own game, let us not forget that they were also playing a major part in winning the hearts and minds of the local people and establishing friendly contacts with the Ibans in the longhouses, at the same time asking them to pass on any news or rumours about the enemy. There were many stories about how the local people were won over to the government's side. After the worst of the Confrontation was over, helicopters were used to help win over the Ibans and one pilot was surprised when a Gurkha base drummer,

clutching his precious drum, had to be roped down through the jungle
to a small clearing below. The Ibans were even more amazed when
the sound of bagpipes was heard and the throb of military drums
resounded through the trees and undergrowth. It did not take long
for them to reciprocate with their own songs and dances and the
final mixture included Scottish reels, Iban dances, Malay ronggeng,
Nepali nautches and even a version of the Western 'Twist'.

At the height of the Confrontation, and before cross-border operations were authorized politically, the Security Forces were hard-
pressed to cope with the wide range of options open to the Indonesians
from their various bases. In the First Division of Sarawak, in particular, the threat was a very real one, so that in time strongly defended
platoon patrol bases were set up at approximately six-mile intervals.
These varied in size and shape and were not unlike Beau Geste forts,
with sandbag emplacements, overhead cover, protected sleeping
accommodation, as well as an ingenious and deadly array of electri-
cally detonated explosives in various positions outside the perimeter.
Each fort or base had its own mortars and a few of them had 105
millimetre guns as well.

These forts were not built for static defence but were intended to
form firm bases for aggressive patrolling forward to the border as
well as linking up with troops on both flanks. The Gurkha Engineer
squadrons played a large part in setting up the bases. In addition,
they made sapper history in January, 1964, when, after being lifted
by a Belvedere helicopter sixty-five miles into the jungle, C Troop of
69 Gurkha Independent Field Squadron took delivery of a bulldozer
and started to construct the first medium-range transport strip built
in those surroundings. It was no easy task because at the outset heavy
rains fell for days, but by using local tribesmen (Kelabits) as labour,
the assignment was duly completed on schedule. Another unusual
duty was to take over the running of river launches and longboats
from the Royal Navy. Where the outboards were of the civilian
type used by the local fishermen, then the motors were reliable—as
opposed to some types produced by the Services which became the
target of much abuse by the Gurkha sapper boatmen!

Although the Gurkha Engineers had many glamorous tasks to
fulfil, as far as the Infantry battalions were concerned their gratitude
was centred on the efforts made by the sappers to improve living
conditions in the forward bases. These included the construction of
water points which, in time, meant welcome showers, even to the

extent of having the luxury of hot water. The list of works completed by the Gurkha sappers embraces a wide variety of projects such as constructing a police station, building village jetties, and even clearing a river with explosives after it had become blocked with tree trunks during the floods. Cutting LZs for helicopters naturally produced several tense moments, especially when Indonesian infiltrators were known to be in the area. If it can be said that the Gurkha Engineers learnt to walk during the Malayan Emergency, then in Borneo they came of age. They left the country a better place because by their efforts they had helped to open up many parts of Borneo by improving airstrips and river communications, and by building permanent roads into the interior.

Whereas the Gurkha Engineers could point to their achievements—the roads, bases and airfields—it was not easy for the Gurkha Signals to demonstrate what they had done, so efficiently, throughout the Confrontation. Two out of the three Brigade Signal Squadrons of the Regiment served continuously in Borneo, providing reliable communications which enabled the Security Forces to maintain the initiative in some of the most difficult country in the world. That the movement of Indonesian columns when they crossed the border was known almost instantaneously was due in no small measure to the communications run and maintained by the Gurkha Signals. Perhaps their most remarkable achievement was to establish VHF re-broadcast facilities on some of the highest peaks, one of them being nearly 8,000 feet. Here the radio relay detachments lived in complete isolation, wholly dependent on visiting helicopters which brought in stores and rations, as well as enabling the personnel manning the station to be changed round. Even after huts had been built to house the men and equipment on the 8,000 foot peak, it was a far from pleasant spot to live and work in, so the operators were changed round at fortnightly intervals. This and other re-broadcast sites ensured that there were VHF communications throughout the Brigade areas, a remarkable achievement which, of course, could never have been brought about without the helicopters which were used at all stages, for cutting the initial LZ, establishing the party, flying in their precious equipment, and thereafter keeping the post resupplied to meet the operational requirements.

The Gurkha Signals have an amusing story to tell. While in the Kuching area they were presented with six bicycles by courtesy of a grant from the Nuffield Trust. The Trust administrators asked for a letter of thanks as well as an 'action photo' so that the trustees could see how their grant had been spent. Six Gurkhas were duly paraded in day mufti and told to mount the bicycles. Unfortunately only three of them could ride a bicycle. The QGO ordered the hand pumps to be removed and the Nuffield Trust now have a photograph of six Gurkha Signallers pumping up bicycle tyres, their smiles hiding the fact that three of them could not use the machines!

The Gurkha Transport Regiment—redesignated thus in November, 1965, when the companies became squadrons—had 30 and 31 Squadrons, in turn, carrying out tours in Borneo before they moved back to Singapore in January, 1967. As the tempo of operations increased, they had detachments dispersed over a thousand miles, in places as far apart as the capital, Kuching, the island of Labuan and Tawau away to the east. Their composite platoons gave magnificent support to the troops operating in their vicinity, while in the rear the transport platoons worked round the clock ferrying stores from airfields and docks, as well as moving units and sub-units to and from operations. And unlike the other units, whose tasks came to a close when Confrontation ended in August, 1966, the Gurkha Transport Regiment reported that 'in four months we moved back from the forward areas; the ports and airfields, every soldier and ton of stores it had taken us three years to bring forward'.

Until political clearance for cross-border operations was given, President Sukarno had every chance of winning an outright victory which would have meant the end of the fledgling Federation of Malaysia. Even after the successful conclusion of the Borneo campaign, a great deal of unnecessary secrecy was attached to the cross-border operations that had taken place. It is not necessary to go into any detail except to affirm that the Gurkhas hit the Indonesians hard by methods which neither escalated the war nor invited the United Nations to intervene. In a campaign where there was no area bombing, no napalm or defoliation of the jungle, it was no wonder that the Commonwealth Forces were welcomed for the benefits they brought to the longhouses. By mastering the physical conditions, by securing the willing help of the inhabitants and by the skilful use of thoroughly trained infantrymen, the campaign was won without the people at home or the world at large realizing the extent of the fighting soldiers' achievements.

There was a long list of decorations for valour given to the Brigade during the campaign, at the top of which was Lance-Corporal Rambahadur Limbu of the 10th Gurkha Rifles who won the VC not—as the citation at the time alleged—for repulsing an Indonesian raid within Sarawak but for his bravery on one of the highly successful cross-border raids that turned defeat into victory.

Rambahadur Limbu was still serving in 1983, as a Captain (QGO), when he was selected to become one of the Queen's Gurkha Orderly Officers, to be in attendance on Her Majesty at the investitures held in Buckingham Palace. He was also a popular guest at many functions all over the UK. Some time before this he visited Canada with five Gurkha Pipe Majors to raise funds for the Gurkha Welfare Trust. In Toronto one sunny day he and the Pipe Majors were entertained by good friends of the Gurkhas and in the garden, after lunch, the daughter of the house, who had recently visited Nepal, produced a cheap bamboo flute which she had brought back. The five Edinburgh-trained Pipe Majors were invited to play it. Each tried and failed. Then she passed it to Rambahadur Limbu VC. With a diffident smile he raised it to his lips and suddenly the sunlit pergola was filled with the sound of the pipes of Pan. Giving the flute back to its owner, Rambahadur said, 'You see, instead of going to school I minded the goats and played the flute all day!'

The shooting war came to an end in 1966. Negotiations to end the Confrontation had been started by Indonesia and Malaysia and nothing was being done by the Commonwealth Security Forces which could be interpreted as provocative. Contact was made at several points along the border, especially between the Penghulus (headmen) and their counterparts in Kalimantan, with the aim of restoring the friendly relationships of the pre-Confrontation era. One British company commander near the border received the following letter:

Dear Honourable Fellow Soldier,
A unit associated with the TNI wishes to fire the border with mortars. Please do not send your people on patrol to the border. We are both looking for Communists and in the same way we are Anti-Communists.
Secondly, I thank you very much for your last firing:
I am very glad for this first letter which I write between our units. Thank you very much and I hope you will reply to this letter as soon as possible.
That's all, thank you.

Signed Sergeant Major Sjakur.
Post Commander Lian Tuar. Dated 27.6.66

This was followed a few days later by thirty-six packets of Indonesian cigarettes, two bars of soap and a further letter.

Dear Commander Post Ba Kelalan,
With this letter I enclose some cigarettes from outside stock. The reason we send these cigarettes to the Commander Post Ba Kelalan is for an exchange of your own cigarettes. So that we may both have a different taste.
In conclusion I thank you very much.
From the Post Ba Bawan.
Signed Sjakur (Sergeant Major).

Unfortunately, the order at that time was that there was to be no fraternization with the enemy until negotiations had been completed, so the cigarettes and bars of soap were returned by post!

After the agreement had been signed the Confrontation should have ended, but reports began seeping in about a man feared by the local people, Lieutenant Sumbi. Sumbi was said to be training about 100 volunteers in jungle warfare and had been boasting that, one day, he and his men would cross the border, march on Brunei Bay, and from there seize the Shell Oil installations in Seria. Then, from the same defended post that had refused to exchange cigarettes, Ba Kelalan, a definite report was received that Sumbi had moved out from Long Bawang in Kalimantan for 'an unknown destination'. A massive search operation was put into effect, which would have been like looking for a needle in a haystack had it not been for a rifleman in the Gurkha Parachute Company. While on patrol he came across a piece of tinfoil which had been trodden into the ground and smelt of coffee. He realized that no one in the vicinity, native or serviceman, drank coffee, so he, and the sergeant accompanying him, cast about for three hours and eventually found a disused camp fire about half a mile away. The search operation moved into top gear and the hunt for Sumbi was on. He gave them quite a chase. Indeed, Sumbi himself was not captured for six weeks. By that time some troops had been winched down into the remote mountainous areas and it was to take some two weeks of cliff-hanging, crossing many rivers and meticulous tracking before the final group of Sumbi's volunteers were eliminated, captured or, like Sumbi himself, decided to surrender. Sumbi refused to talk in spite of some expert interrogation. Then a QGO gave him some Gurkha rum and *in vino* the tough Indonesian began to bare his soul and his secrets.

As soon as the Confrontation was over, messages of praise and congratulation poured in at the same time as rumours began to appear in the British Press that a large-scale reduction in the Brigade was about to be announced by the Labour Government of the day.

Such a situation had faced Major-General Walker when he took over as MGBG before the Confrontation. In 1962 General Walker had risked the extreme displeasure of his superiors by the stand that he had taken on the future of the Gurkha Brigade in the British Army. To him it had been of more importance to make every effort to save the Brigade from crippling reductions—which might lead to eventual disbandment—than to abide by protocol or worry about his own future. Fortunately for the whole Brigade, including General Walker, such plans as there were had to be shelved when the revolt broke out in Brunei.

Now his successor as MGBG, Major-General A. G. (Pat) Patterson, faced a similar situation and once again it was an anxious time for all ranks. General Patterson, a man of great integrity, fought with wholehearted determination to negotiate reasonable terms for the men he led with respect and affection. Before the rundown was publicly announced to all ranks of the Brigade during December, 1966, the MGBG had briefed his Commanding Officers for the daunting task that was soon to face them all, that of sending over half the Brigade on redundancy prematurely, including many without any type of pension, and with only a small gratuity.

Certain important principles were evolved by General Patterson, later to be accepted *in toto* by the Ministry of Defence in London, and without doubt these paved the way for the difficult and heartrending business of sending home volunteer 'long-term' regular soldiers. One of these principles was a public announcement that each year there would be limited recruiting; the General was demonstrating his faith in the future as well as ensuring that the Brigade would have the correct rank structure, if it continued as part of the British Army during and beyond the 1970s. Events were to prove him right in every respect.

The official announcement was made simultaneously in December by all Commanding Officers throughout the Brigade. There had been so much speculation and so many rumours that the actual announcement did not come as much of a shock. As one CO was to write:

> It was all done very quietly, without fuss and strain or any sense of drama. I personally briefed British and Gurkha Officers in their respective messes and the company commanders then briefed their men in the company lines. It was kept to a very low key and on the whole the men took the news very philosophically. The result was that they found it very interesting but they didn't really expect it to affect them, and if it did—well that was life!

Another example of Gurkha fatalism. What will be, will be.

In the event, there were remarkably few disgruntled men to be sent on redundancy, thanks to the careful preparation, meticulous briefing and deep personal interest taken in every case by the British and Gurkha officers in each unit.

By the original 1966 plan, the four infantry regiments were to have been reduced to a single battalion each by the end of 1971. However, in the middle of 1970 two events occurred in the United Kingdom. Firstly, the situation in Northern Ireland worsened so that more British troops were required in a hurry, and secondly, the Conservative Party emerged as surprise victors in the General Election. It would be unfair to put too much emphasis on the second factor, since it is more than possible that the situation in Northern Ireland would have influenced a Labour administration into making the same decision about the Brigade as did the new Government. Be that as it may, the formal announcement about the Brigade's future came from the Ministry of Defence when it was stated, quite categorically, that the Brigade would not be run down below an overall strength of 6,700 Gurkha ranks and that this total would include five Infantry battalions as well as three small but viable Gurkha Corps.

The decision was of far-reaching significance and everyone was delighted that some 700 more men would continue to serve for the foreseeable future. It meant, too, that the senior infantry regiment, the 2nd Gurkhas, continued on a two-battalion basis—unlike the other three regiments which now consisted of a single battalion. The three Corps, too, could now plan for a definite future in the Brigade.

The battle for existence had been won and a further step forward was taken in 1982 when a modest but most welcome expansion was announced which led to the 2/7th Gurkha Rifles being reformed and re-titled in February of that year. In addition, 69 Gurkha Independent Field Squadron after an all-too-brief existence of seven years, most of which had been spent in Borneo, was reformed in Hong Kong prior to moving to Chatham in the UK. Here the Squadron has taken on the same tasks as any Royal Engineer field squadron, including a tour in the Falklands.

The Brigade of Gurkhas during the 1970s had found that its fortunes had changed from an uncertain future to an assured place in the British Army, and Gurkha battalions have since been used in several 'war in peace' situations throughout the world. Towards the end of the 1960s four Gurkha battalions were engaged in keeping the peace along the Hong Kong–Chinese border outstaring the Red Guards and conducting internal security duties in the urban area.

The Gurkhas were not popular with everyone during this phase. It was inevitable that the Communist Press would turn its attention to 'the mercenary Gurkhas helping the reactionary British' and typical comments on two incidents read as follows:

The Wolf Police and the Beast Troops encircled half the area. The British Troops aimed their guns at the inhabitants. In spite of being armed to the teeth they were very much afraid of being counter-attacked. The Gurkhas back to back, pressed each other hard on one side ... They pointed their guns at the pedestrians, the shops and the tenants above. The masses who faced the Beast soldiers and Wolf Policemen were without fear and withdrew safely.

Splendid words, especially as, in the second incident, only one Landrover with a small escort was involved. It was summed up aptly by a young British officer who commented, 'If they can believe that trash, then the unfortunates can believe anything!'

When the heat had been taken out of the Chinese frontier problem, the next task, lasting several more years, was to try and prevent the trickle of illegal immigrants from across the border turning into a flood. The climax was reached in mid-1979 when nearly 90,000 illegal immigrants were arrested, by which time five battalions had been deployed along the border. Without their vigilance the already over-crowded colony would have been swamped.

Away from Hong Kong in 1974, the 10th Gurkha Rifles flew to Cyprus from Church Crookham in an operational role and found themselves back at the familiar task of running road blocks, searching vehicles and carrying out other internal security duties while trying to prevent the Greek Cypriots from attacking the Turkish community, and vice versa. Here the Gurkhas won warm praise for their calmness, efficiency and friendly attitude to both sections of the population, and their presence in the island helped to stabilize an extremely dangerous situation.

Then it was the turn of the 6th Gurkha Rifles to be whisked away from Church Crookham, this time to Belize on a seven-month emergency tour. Belize was known as British Honduras until 1975 and the newly independent country was being threatened by Guatemala, her big neighbour. Here the Gurkhas found the jungles far more dense and inhospitable than the ones they had grown accustomed to in Borneo and Malaya; nevertheless, the old skills quickly returned and since then the other infantry battalions of the Brigade have served operational tours in Belize, their presence in the small garrison serving to act as a deterrent to the Guatemalans.

Having a battalion serving in the UK, usually on a two-year tour, albeit without their wives and children, has proved popular with the Brigade. Apart from giving the Gurkha soldiers a chance to see the UK and to get away from the rather claustrophobic atmosphere of Hong Kong, while serving in this country the QGOs and men draw the same rates of pay as their equivalent rank in the British infantry. Not unnaturally, this is a big incentive. By prudent saving they can return to Nepal in a position to buy a plot of land or a house, something that would have been impossible in the past except for the senior Gurkha Officers.

That they are popular wherever they go in England, Scotland or Wales goes without saying. Northern Ireland is 'off-limits' for political reasons and as the situation there confuses the average British soldier, it is just as well that the Hindu Gurkha is not asked to stand between factions who profess to be followers of the same Christ.

Not everyone who sees the Gurkhas on Public Duties in London knows who they are, as these comments overheard by a British officer indicate. While a Gurkha guard was taking over from the Guards, someone shouted out: 'Who are they?'

Another bystander replied 'Know the tall ones—them's the Guards, don't know who the other lot are!'

However, a few minutes later the officer's morale rose when another hoarse voice shouted at the Guards: 'You blokes want to wake your ideas up. Those little chaps are making you look like a bunch of amateurs.'

Even the gentlemen of the Press can be fooled by the Mongolian features. One of their representatives said politely to an officer who was watching two of his pipers preparing to go on parade: 'Excuse me, I'm from the Press. Could you tell me what these two Oriental gentlemen are doing blowing their pipes there?'

As the Pipe Major was one of the Oriental gents, he was not amused!

Running Bisley each year has brought the UK-based battalion into the public eye and each unit, in turn, has won warm praise for the way affairs have been organized. On occasions there can still be a few language problems as an officer found out when talking to an NCO on butt duty on the range.

The Gurkha asked: 'Where do you come from, Sahib?'

'I come from Devon.'

'Ah, Heaven, Sahib, I know.'

'No, not Heaven—Devon. It is a county in England.'

A pause, a wide smile before the confident assertion: 'I know, Sahib; I know Heaven.'

Perhaps that is why one regiment is called 'The God's Own Goorkhas'.

With a Gurkha battalion stationed at Church Crookham continuously over the last thirteen or fourteen years, the question is often asked: how is their discipline affected by the higher rates of pay and the fact that for a period of 24 months the Gurkha officers and men are without their families? It would be dishonest to claim that any battalion, serving a two-year tour, does so without some problems, because the temptations are there and as has been said before, the average Gurkha likes his 'wine, women and song', especially at festival time. That the cases of severe ill-discipline are few and far between can be put down to several factors.

Perhaps the biggest deterrent is the threat that anyone who brings his regiment's name into disrepute will find himself on the next available aircraft back to Hong Kong, and usually after he has been given a more normal military punishment. Such a dramatic exodus serves as a most effective deterrent because the man automatically loses his UK rates of pay, the one chance perhaps in his whole service when he can save the sort of money required to buy a modest house or a plot of land back home. Added to the financial loss is the fact that he can bid farewell to any chance of further promotion; certain it is that his officers will never forgive his misdemeanour. Or more accurately, even if the British officers were to relent, the Gurkha officers would not forget, let alone advocate a pardon.

Although fear of such drastic punishment undoubtedly influences those soldiers who have a mind to wander from the straight and narrow path, the majority behave themselves because it is in their blood, in their upbringing, and to get a 'badnam' is viewed as something akin to death by the average soldier, brought up as he is to obey his superiors in age and rank. One amusing misdemeanour is worth recording because it ended on a note of comedy, thanks to some tactful handling by a British officer. For obvious reasons the names of individuals and regiments are not revealed. One night the adjutant of the resident UK Gurkha Battalion was woken up by a telephone call from a nearby police station.

'Sorry to call you at this late hour, sir, but we have a Gurkha in custody. He was driving under the influence of drink so we took him in before he had an accident. He refuses to say anything except to give his number, rank and name. Can I ask you to come over, sir?'

The Adjutant agreed, dressed quickly and drove to the police station where he found that the Gurkha did not belong to his unit; he recognized him as a sergeant from another regiment, who was on a course in the UK.

The NCO stood up respectfully when the Adjutant entered and spoke in Gurkhali: 'Don't worry, Sahib, I haven't given them any information except my number, rank and name.' He was obviously drunk but not belligerent, or at least so the Adjutant thought until the man continued speaking, fortunately still in Gurkhali: 'Sahib, you tackle the big policeman and I'll go for the short one. If we do it together we can get out of this POW camp.' When the policeman asked what the Gurkha had said, the Adjutant quickly replied that he was apologizing for causing trouble and would go quietly into military custody in the realization that he would be dealt with strictly and promptly by his officers. The police agreed to release him—especially as they had his number, rank and name—and the pair walked quietly out of the station. In due course, the NCO was punished but as no harm had occurred and he was an excellent soldier with bright prospects ahead the matter ended in smiles.

The biggest challenge to any Gurkha battalion since the end of the Confrontation was to come in May, 1982 when the 1/7th Duke of Edinburgh's Own Gurkha Rifles left Church Crookham, bound for

Southampton where they embarked on the *Queen Elizabeth II en route* for the Falklands. They were given a rapturous send-off by thousands of people who had made their way to the docks. The Ministry of Defence could not have chosen taller shipmates for the Gurkhas: two battalions from the Brigade of Guards were their companions as part of 5 Brigade. The Gurkhas set sail full of trepidation about possible seasickness which, as landlocked mountain dwellers, they treat with the utmost seriousness.

The beginning was shrouded in doubts. As one officer wrote:

> Until we actually sailed I think most of us thought we would never go . . . there were fears that we, as a Gurkha battalion, might not be allowed to go to the Falkland Islands for political reasons. In the event these fears proved unfounded and the Nepalese Government responded as it had done on many previous occasions by signifying its complete support of the British Government.

Let us leave the senior officers, the war correspondents, and military commentators as they voice their opinions, often heavily laden with the benefits of hindsight, and look at the story of the Falklands as told by Rifleman Baliprasad Rai in the Brigade newspaper *Parbate* on 22 July. The original was translated into English by Sgt Jasbahadur Gurung and was headed, 'From Bagsila to Bluff Cove' ('A soldier's story of the Falklands War'). It began in this way: 'From the hills of Sagarmatha to the seas of the South Atlantic is a long way, but I have travelled it and what a trip it has been!'

The story starts when Baliprasad was enlisted at Dharan in April, 1980, and within a short space of time, 'We were turned from raw recruits into trained soldiers by our instructors at Sek Kong'. He was posted to the 7th Gurkha Rifles where he was sent to the Pipes and Drums Platoon, 'possibly due to my preference for music. It was not all blowing the bagpipes though, as our Platoon also doubled as the GMG Platoon' (more accurately, GPMG, General Purpose Machine Gun).

His battalion moved to England for a two-year tour in March, 1981, about which the Rifleman was to comment:

> Our barracks at Church Crookham was old, but comfortable inside and I found the people friendly. We were kept busy since our arrival with various commitments . . . and numerous band shows

to perform all over the country, but it was a good and fairly cheap way of seeing Britain!

Not surprisingly, the young Rifleman had an adverse comment to make about the

bitterly cold English winter when I had my first taste of real snow. I thought that whatever Bagsila's shortcomings, it was never as cold as this. Little did I know that this was nothing compared to what I was to endure.

Then came the warning order to move to the South Atlantic and there was a different atmosphere in camp, 'electric you might say!' Everything from extra equipment to Arctic clothing was issued, including huge, heavy rucksacks to carry all the kit in.

These rucksacks when packed looked even larger than some of us! . . . it was an exhausting time. Many television and newspaper reporters were in camp to film our activity and we obliged them by posing with our unsheathed kukris—to put the fear of the Gurkhas into the Argentines!

Psychological warfare had begun and the passing days would show that it was totally effective. Rifleman Baliprasad Rai was attached to 'B' Company as their GPMG detachment gunner. After three days' holiday in London which was

enough for me and my pocket I returned to camp relaxed and refreshed and eager for anything. '*Je hola hola*' (whatever will be, will be) was the general concensus of opinion. Our forefathers had earned us our enviable reputation and we were proud of our name. But it is not enough to let the name honour us, we must honour the name. And here was the chance to do it.

The last night in Church Crookham before embarkation was 'a funfilled night in the Junior Ranks Club. Hardly anyone slept—we were all there, sitting, talking, drinking, dancing and making jokes'. At six o'clock in the morning they were ready to move down to Southampton where Baliprasad recorded 'literally thousands of people lining the streets of Southampton, all cheering and waving as we passed by on our way to the docks, and I think no one could help feeling a little warmth in their hearts.'

Like his fellow riflemen, he was astounded at the size of the *Queen Elizabeth II*:

> Such a ship had to be seen to be believed. Why, it was even larger than any building I'd seen back home . . . Never had I slept in such beautiful surroundings or in such a big, soft bed, nor perhaps I ever will! If I was to go to war, then there was no better way to go.

Thereafter he was to find that life on the *QE II* was much the same as in the Queen Elizabeth Barracks, near Aldershot.

> BFT [Basic Fitness Training] in the morning to keep us physically fit followed by lessons in skill-at-arms. We even learned to fire the .50″ Browning machine-gun and live firings with our personal weapons were often held using empty ammunition boxes as targets. . . . Hundreds of Hindi and English video films provided recreation in the evenings and on the whole voyage I must have seen *Desh Premee* at least ten times!

On the whole, life on the *QE II* was pleasant, especially as there was no seasickness among the Gurkhas. This happy state was soon to change when the Battalion transferred from the big liner on to the ferry ship *Norland* where, dressed in their full complement of Arctic gear, they swayed, shook and rolled towards the East Falklands.

> It was only about 800 miles away they said to me but to me it seemed to be 80,000 miles as my bowels remained in a constant state of turmoil and no amount of seasick tablets could settle it. . . . All around me I could see the same scenes, people huddled against the cold and the wind, straining to gain some semblance of balance as we were bounced and buffetted like rag dolls. I would have willingly sat through hours of Argentine torture than go through another minute of this ordeal!

After that long tiring journey they landed at Port San Carlos where the order to dig in was given, just in time:

> We dived into our freshly dug holes before the first wave of

Argentine aircrafts swooped in very low over the hills ... All the weapons from the ground forces attacked these Argentine jets ... What a spectacular show it was, a spectacle never to be forgotten and I don't think I ever will. The full and harsh realism of war was upon us.

The 1/7th Gurkhas moved to Goose Green and spent many hours climbing in and out of helicopters to scour the East Falkland hills for pockets of enemy believed to be hiding there. Baliprasad was not impressed with the positions they found abandoned by their enemy.

Their trenches were always poorly dug, inadequately sheltered with only a tin sheet or a tarpaulin overhead and a couple of blankets below. Some even had webbing, clothing and various oddments of war in them. We could only shake our heads in wonder at the sheer waste.

For the young Gurkha soldier, this was an understandable reaction, against all his training and the way he had been brought up in Bagsila. Such items would never be discarded in the hills—everything that can be used is hoarded against a rainy day.

For a few days it was the weather that had become the enemy, with rain, mist and low clouds adding to the gloom.

All our kit and clothing were soaked and remained soaked, and the icy winds of the Antarctic would chill us to the bone no matter how many woolies we wore. It was colder and wetter than ten English winters combined and they said this was just the starters!

By good fortune the 7th Gurkhas just missed the terrible fate that befell the Welsh Guardsmen at Bluff Cove.

On 9 June, the Battalion, less 'C' Company, began to move forward on foot, a distance of about seven kilometres over extremely rough ground. The marching was hard, no one was lightly laden, but those with the extra burdens to carry, such as the Milan firing-posts or like, Baliprasad, GPMG (SF) tripods, found things none too easy. To make matters worse the Gurkhas were spotted by the Argentinians and a fierce mortar barrage followed. 'The night sky was lit with flares like the many times I'd seen an exercise—only this time it was for real!' The following day the barrage became more intense as the

Gurkhas were in full view of Argentine observers on Mount Harriet. Shells began to fall on them: mercifully they came only singly but they were big ones, 155 mm. 'B' Company was hardest hit:

> It was increasingly difficult to poke our heads above the trench, crouched as we were in waist-deep muddy water. The shells whistled and whined above our heads and crashed around with a deafening noise, showering everyone with dirt. ... The shells seemed to come even closer and I'd not be telling the truth if I said I was not at all frightened. I thoroughly was but I was also angry. This is no way to fight a fight I thought and a No. 1 gunner was no use in this situation no matter how good.... I heard my trench-mate, Lance-Corporal Gyanendra Rai, cry out. He had been hit by flying shrapnel on his shoulder. I told him, 'There is blood pouring down your back'. He looked at me and replied, 'You are also hit. There is blood all over the back of your head.' Yes, a piece of shrapnel had penetrated my tin hat and lodged itself in the back of my head. Only then did I feel the pain.

The Company Second in Command, Captain (QGO) Dalbahadur Sunwar, and three riflemen had been hit and they were evacuated back to San Carlos where the large sheep-shearing station at the settlement had been turned into a field hospital. It was crowded with Guardsmen, Paratroopers and even Argentinian wounded, who lay about as teams of medical men and doctors worked on them. Thus did the rifleman describe the scene, adding that:

> I had the dubious distinction of being the first Gurkha casualty to be taken there. I did not have to stay long because the next day I was put on to the hospital ship *Uganda*. I do not remember much about it except for the care and the warmth of the many nurses and doctors who looked after me. I constantly thought about my friends in 'B' Company and what they were going through with, and I wished I could go back to them.

But Baliprasad was evacuated back to England and the story ends before his battalion returned to join him:

> As I relax and enjoy my sick leave here my mind retraces the long journey I have made—from the quiet stillness of Bagsila to the

blood and thunder of the bombardment of Bluff Cove. Yes, it has
been an incredible journey—and yes, I have been lucky again.

Meanwhile back in the Falklands, the Battalion waited for new
orders, patiently remaining in reserve until 13 June when they were
flown by helicopter to a point just south of the Two Sisters feature;
it was here that they were given orders for their part in 5 Brigade's
attack on Tumbledown and Mount William, which was due to begin
just after midnight on 14 June. An officer wrote: 'Listening to the
preparatory bombardment on that night of 13/14 June made one feel
really glad to be British! Five batteries of 105 mm guns and several
Royal Navy ships fired in support of the Brigade, all of which was
very reassuring for us.' Most of the night was spent moving forward
very slowly in fits and starts; the weather was atrocious with strong
winds and frequent snow showers as the unit followed the Scots
Guards who had been ordered to secure Tumbledown *en route*. At
the appropriate moment the 1/7th Gurkhas were to pass through the
Scots Guards, swing right and assault and capture Mount William.

In extremely difficult country, moving slowly in single file, with
illuminating shells of all kinds lighting up the sky and tracer criss-
crossing the hills in front of them, the Battalion was nearing its start-
point when part of the column was hit by enemy DF (Defensive Fire).
Fortunately, the soft nature of the ground saved countless lives and
later it was found that only eight men of the Battalion had been hit.
It was a long and frustrating night as they waited for the order which
would release them to pass through the Scots Guards and take Mount
William. A minefield was discovered through which a lane had to be
cleared, although it was later learnt that the whole of another company
had passed through the same minefield without casualties. It was at
such a time, raring to go after a night of frustration, delay and fear,
that white flags were seen flying over Port Stanley. The Second-in-
Command, Major Bill Dawson, achieved temporary fame when he
appeared on the TV screen, with the remark that will not be forgotten
by his fellow officers: 'There is a white flag flying over Stanley. Bloody
Marvellous: Tee Hee!'

Not surprisingly, the officers and men who had taken part in that
night advance felt thoroughly dispirited, even cheated. It was not
because they were thirsty for blood or the chance to prove the stories
circulating among the Argentinians concerning the Gurkhas and their
kukris. Rather was it that having travelled so far they were not given

an opportunity to show the world that they could do as well as their British comrades on the Falklands, or even better!

The Commanding Officer wrote shortly afterwards:

We found a host of dead and empty enemy trenches. It was most frustrating, but I am absolutely certain that they knew (a) they were outflanked when they saw this line of men coming towards them, and they couldn't do anything about it and (b) they also knew they had not yet come up against the Gurkhas, and told us that they were 'dreadfully worried and scared' of meeting us.

When the war was over the Argentinians paid their own 'tribute' to the Gurkhas and their fearsome reputation. One report claimed that when 300 Argentinians fled from the Scots Guards, they ran into the Gurkhas' advance patrols, whereupon they immediately turned and ran back to surrender to the Guards. A few days later the most extraordinary allegations appeared in the Argentine Press, one claiming that the Gurkhas killed their own wounded rather than let them be taken by an enemy in action. Another claimed that the Gurkhas went into action 'drunk and high on drugs'. Such statements caused much amusement in HQ 5 Brigade, under whose command the 1/7th Gurkhas had been. A spokesman at 5 Brigade said: 'None of these things ever happened, of course, but the Gurkhas don't mind. It has added to their reputation in battle—it will help when and if there is another enemy to fight.'

In spite of the stress and strains of battle, there was still a chance to smile. Early one morning, the CO temporarily dislocated his shoulder when pulling on his long rubber overboots. He said to his orderly, Lance-Corporal Dilbahadur Rai, 'Quickly, go and get the doctor'. The orderly ran to where the Command Post was set up, burst in and shouted, 'Where's the Doctor Sahib? The Commanding Sahib has been bitten by a snake'. Such imagination impressed everybody! By the time the doctor was found, the CO's shoulder was back in place and all was well.

There was also a quip made by the Gurkha Major to Major Dawson one morning after the operation was over and the Battalion had been low on rations for some time. *Shikar* (hunting) was organized to help to improve the menu. Inevitably, this meant some loss for the civilians at Goose Green and, following a particularly successful hunting trip, the Gurkha Major commented wryly: 'If this goes on much longer they will have to re-name Goose Green just Green!'

So, after rumour and counter-rumour, it was back to the UK for the 1/7th Gurkha Rifles. The Battalion received a heartwarming reception, especially from the people of Fleet who took the opportunity to express their appreciation, not only of the Battalion's part in the Falklands campaign but their excellent discipline and immaculate behaviour while stationed at nearby Church Crookham. It was typical of the professional attitude of the Brigade that at a time when there was considerable national and military euphoria about the success of the British Forces in the South Atlantic, the Commanding Officer sounded a warning in a paper, from which the following is an extract.

> There is a danger that the success of the British tactics in the Falklands may bring about a dangerous over-confidence. It must be clearly understood that generally the enemy were of inferior quality. They made many elementary mistakes such as:
> > Not covering minefields with fire
> > Not carrying out aggressive patrolling
> > Not executing a single counter-attack
> > Not using any defence stores
> The list is not exhaustive!

Wise words with which many would agree!

The next battalion to arrive in the UK, the 10th Gurkha Rifles, has completed a tour in Belize, as have 69 Gurkha Field Squadron, and this commitment is likely to be handed on to their successors. In addition, the Gurkha Engineers have had troops down in the Falklands engaged on the extremely dangerous task of lifting up minefields and booby traps, many of which had not been recorded or marked by the Argentinians.

Those who do not understand the Brigade, or the close relationship between Britain and Nepal, sometimes maintain that the Gurkhas are a mercenary force, that the concept is out of date and the Brigade should be disbanded. Harka Gurung, a former Nepalese Cabinet member whose father and two older brothers were Gurkha soldiers under the British Crown, was asked this question. He replied:

> My clan, the Gurungs, have always liked serving with the British

because they earned rank on the basis of merit or bravery, not social status or position . . . The Nepalese do realize it is a hangover from a colonial era that reflects on Nepal's past, perhaps. Among leftists, it is an issue. For the groups who get economic benefits, it is not important.

With about 20 per cent of hard-pressed Nepal's foreign exchange coming from Britain's Brigade of Gurkhas, together with its variety of projects and other sponsored work, neither the present King, nor the British Government, is unhappy with the system. Time has not run out for a tradition embodying concepts of honour and duty that have never been tarnished. A British officer once advised that, 'Anyone who wants to understand the meaning of courage and selflessness should soldier with a Gurkha Regiment. He will return an enlightened and a better man.'

EIGHT

Festivals and Folk Lore

The Gurkhas are Hindus, says the official handbook, a statement which is about as accurate as saying that all British are Christians. Officially Nepal is a Hindu kingdom but as any visitor to Kathmandu can see, there is a strong Buddhist influence in many of its temples. The neighbouring old city of Patan, some two miles from Kathmandu, was essentially a Buddhist city; there are many relics of that faith, relics because it suffered severely when Prithwi Narayan and his warriors from Gorkha conquered the Valley way back in 1767.

Away from the Valley, there are several places where Buddhism holds sway: in the Sherpa country around Namchhe and wherever there are pockets of displaced Tibetans who have settled in Nepal, for example in the small hamlet of Hile above Dhankutta. Centuries ago, it is certain that the warlike Rais and Limbus of East Nepal, who serve in the 7th and 10th Gurkha Rifles as they have done from the early days of both those Regiments, came from Tibet. Indeed, the language of the Limbus is of the Tibetan group. When Rais and Limbus are recruited into the British Army, their religion is shown on all personal documents as being Hindu. In a sense this is done in deference to the Hindu kingdom in which they live: many would claim that the majority of the Eastern Nepal tribes are indifferent to religion, mumbling the 'Om Mane Padme Hum' as Buddhists do when it suits them, and consulting the local Brahmin priest on other occasions. It is fair to say that the average Gurkha soldier, like his British counterpart, turns to religion when faced with impending death or disaster or when he is overcome by fear of the future. The oft-hard-drinking Sherpa porters still say a prayer, or place a humble offering beside the idol adjoining the mountain track, before setting foot on a rickety swaying suspension bridge which they suspect has not been maintained since its construction (usually, an accurate assumption!).

Ask them why such a gesture is necessary and they will answer with a broad grin: 'Sahib, it does not cost anything, and it has worked every time so far!' On hearing this, the sahib surreptitiously crosses himself, something he has not done in public for years. That works too!

As in the UK, the last decade in Nepal has seen the influence and disciplines of religion diminishing in the lives of a large proportion of the population. Gone are the days when it was mandatory for the Gurkha soldier, on returning from service abroad ('over the Black Water'), to perform a cleansing ceremony, purification from defilement caused by going overseas. The ceremony of absolution, Pani Patiya, lasts for five days, the first of which is a day of complete fasting; thereafter the quantity of rice which may be eaten is increased daily until it reaches a normal ration by the fifth day. Nowadays the ceremony is optional, a state of affairs which is deplored by the unit's *bahun* (priest) because each individual undergoing Pani Patiya is obliged to give a small sum of money to the temple funds.

Nowadays temporarily losing caste by going overseas is treated as a matter of little or no significance by the average Gurkha soldier. To appease those with scruples, they are excused by a charter issued by the Raj Guru from all restrictions as to food except for beef and food known to contain beef extracts. British breakfasts are eaten with gusto by the men stationed in Church Crookham and once they are on active service or full-scale exercises, anything goes. It was not always so, as the following story shows.

During the Malayan Emergency a young Second Lieutenant on almost his first introduction to the jungle was on a long company-sized ambush of some three weeks' duration. During this operation the company was rationed by airdrop about every five days several thousand metres away from the ambush point. After a fortnight the young officer became tired of the Gurkha-type rations and asked through the radio re-supply message for one day's British-type rations for himself. In those days some fresh rations supplemented the compo and were dropped from a Valetta aircraft. Accordingly, together with some still-warm chickens for the Gurkha troops, came a packet of corn flakes, tinned milk, potatoes and about three pounds of prime fillet steak—unfrozen, of course. The subaltern's orderly at that time was a recent enlistment, Rifleman Singbahadur Gurung.

Young Singbahadur took one look at the beef and, in the officer's words, 'his hair stood up'. He then removed all his gear from the sleeping area he shared with his officer and took post on the far side of the Company base. The Company Second-in-Command (a captain QGO) tried to intercede but Singbahadur was adamant. 'Until the Sahib has consumed the beef and the defiled mess tins and cutlery have been exchanged, I will not return to my duties.' For the young Subaltern this was extremely irksome because, after spending twelve hours in the ambush position, it was not only good to be relieved but also to find a hot meal waiting for him. He thought about smoking the meat in order to make it last, but clearly this was not possible if he wanted his orderly back. In the end, he decided there was nothing for it but to consume the beef immediately before it went bad. He offered to share it with the men in the base camp but no one volunteered until it was almost dark when Lieutenant (QGO) Amber-bahadur Gurung came to him in secrecy and said, with feigned reluctance, he would help the officer to eat it, on condition that Rifleman Singbahadur was not told!

Through their combined efforts after dark the beef was finally finished and the mess tins and cutlery were duly exchanged. On the following day, after making a careful scrutiny of the new equipment, Rifleman Singbahadur elected to return to his duties as an orderly, although as a result of this incident, and being a newcomer to the Gurkha Brigade, the Subaltern continued to be wary and respectful of Singbahadur for the few months that he remained as his orderly.

There was an epilogue to this story. Several years later, when Singbahadur had reached the rank of Lance-Corporal, it was Dashera time and the officer, meeting Singbahadur by chance, had a few beers with him to celebrate the festival and their reunion. He recounted the incident of the air-dropped beef, whereupon Singbahadur giggled, saying that he had then been a raw young soldier who had known nothing of life.

'Would you eat beef now?' asked the officer.

'Not by choice,' Singbahadur replied, 'but if there was nothing else available, I would.'

On being asked if he had ever eaten beef he admitted with a smile, 'Yes, at least three times and it tasted good.'

'Do you know who helped me eat the beef that day in the jungle?'

he was asked. Singbahadur shook his head but when Lieutenant (QGO) Amberhadur Gurung arrived to listen to the end of the conversation, the young NCO was helpless with laughter when he heard that a fellow Gurung had been the culprit.

This true story illustrates three important facets of the Gurkhas' character: their pragmatic approach to religious beliefs, sense of humour and ability to laugh at themselves. Their pragmatism can be seen when a Gurkha officer was explaining the difference between the eating habits of the high-caste Chhetris and Brahmins of the Kathmandu valley, whom he disliked, and good, decent Magar-Gurung hillmen like himself. '*They* [the Chhetris/Bahuns] say: perhaps it's beef, I won't eat it; *we* say: perhaps it *isn't* beef, I will eat it.'

Back in the hills of Nepal, however, customs do vary from district to district and each tribe has its own fads which some of the older generation still prefer to observe. Many highlanders will not willingly eat meat from the female of a domestic animal, which is understandable since the females breed when young and are likely to be a tough 'meal' when old. This does not, however, apply to wild game, called *shikar* in Nepali. There are other prejudices which vary from place to place: in West Nepal the Gurungs will not eat tame pig while a neighbouring tribe, the Ghales, will not eat chickens or eggs. In contrast, in East Nepal, we may still find traditional customs such as the eldest son of the family in certain Rai kindreds not being allowed to eat meat after his father has died.

Dashera is the most important Hindu festival of the year, one that is observed with gusto in the hills, the Valley of Kathmandu, and wherever Gurkha soldiers may be serving throughout the world. Dashera is for the Gurkhas what Christmas used to be for us in the United Kingdom before the age of commercialism took over and obliterated so much of its true meaning. Dashera, called by the Nepalese 'Dasain', is a soldier's festival in honour of Durga, Goddess of War. It takes place at the new moon of Asoj (September to October) and lasts for ten days, although in the Army only five of the major feast days are celebrated as holidays. Each day of Dashera has an important religious significance when the priests come into their own, insisting that long-established rituals are carried out to the letter.

To the European observer it is a noisy, cheerful, occasionally drunken and, without mincing words, a bloodthirsty festival. It commemorates two heroic fights: one between Ramchandra and a powerful, evil giant called Rawan; the other between the goddess

Durga and a huge buffalo-headed demon named Mahishashura. On particular days throughout the Dasain festival, various aspects of these two fights are remembered and observed. Durga's fight against the demons raged for six days until, on the seventh day, one of the demon lieutenants was killed. To celebrate this the gods offered flowers and henceforth that festival day became known as Phulpati, the Day of Flowers. On the night of the eighth day Durga fasted and sacrificed a goat; on the next day the goddess was attacked and a fierce combat took place until Durga cut off the attacker's head with her kukri. So much for the religious background, which, for simplicity's sake, has been paraphrased. There is, of course, the happy side to the festival with dancing, feasting and a high consumption of *raksi* (strictly a locally brewed liquor, but the term is often used to cover any type of spirits). Ramchandra also fasted and prayed during the vigil before his day of combat and this is commemorated in the night-long prayers combined with folk dancing, hymns and folk songs known as Kalratri.

It would be idle to pretend that Dashera as celebrated by the modern Brigade conforms in every detail to the celebrations the old Indian Army Brigade enjoyed before India's Independence in 1947. To those officers whose service straddled both eras, the changes from year to year have seemed almost imperceptible. If only to refresh their memories, a report of a typical battalion Dashera of, say, fifty years ago, might have mentioned the following salient features.

For a start, the men's heads would have been shaven, except for a long tuft of hair at the crown, a *tupi*, by which they hoped that their god would pull them up to heaven when they died. The junior ranks would be wearing starched white shorts and white shirts as part of their regimental off-duty dress while on their heads would be a round black hat with the regimental badge in front.

The arms of the battalion have been arranged to form a hollow square on the parade ground, with bayonets fixed and the woodwork of the rifles gleaming dully with jasmine flowers placed in each barrel, while other weapons—automatics, machine guns and cannons won as trophies in the past wars—would be on display nearby.

On the seventh day of the feast, Phulpati, the *bahun* sets out from the barrack heading a procession in which the effigy of Durga is carried, escorted by an armed guard of about fifty men, their rifles loaded with blank ammunition. Behind them a column moves across the countryside, the men collecting flowers as they go. At intervals the armed guard fires a fusillade of 'blanks', a signal for the whole party to call upon the gods to listen to their prayers. On their return to the lines the men place the flowers at the foot of the carved and painted post, the Maula, at which a buffalo will be sacrificed later.

Next day the festivities begin working up to a climax which comes in the evening when groups of soldiers gather about the Maula in a huge semicircle. By now the drummers are beating out a fiery rhythm on their *madals* (drums) and others are singing songs. Young Gurkha soldiers, called Marunis, are dressed up to impersonate women, as Gurkha ladies normally never dance in public. The Marunis are carefully selected for their youth and good looks and many European guests at Dashera parties have been taken in by the surprisingly realistic picture of laughing femininity, with full red and black skirts, embroidered bodices, generous make-up and loose scarves of coloured chiffon draped over their heads.

The Field Security Section (FSS) has also been taken in by the Marunis. Shortly after the 2/7th Gurkha Rifles had celebrated Dashera in 1945 while stationed in Greece, the FSS reported to the Adjutant that five girls had been seen daily in the unit lines. Hasty investigation disclosed that they were the Marunis who had continued their female impersonation at the various company parties throughout the festival. The 'girls' were highly amused, although the Adjutant did not have the heart to enlighten the FSS. Some years later in Malaya a helpful NAAFI manager obtained from the Gurkha Major a list of the items needed for the celebrations. In due course he returned bringing everything except one item which had defeated him. It was 'Seven veils for seven virgins'. What the Gurkha Major wanted was squares of coloured cloth for his Marunis to wear on their heads.

The Marunis' partners, the male dancers, are called Porsenge and during the dance they impersonate the god Krishna, with the Marunis acting as Krishna's milkmaids. The dance, or nautch, still begins with the drummers beating out a lively rhythm on their *madals* while the dancers whirl to the music with ankle bells jingling. The dances vary from regiment to regiment, those of the 7th and 10th Gurkhas being a trifle staid compared with the other battalions in the Brigade, where the audiences are entertained by the more lively tunes from West Nepal.

In years gone by the British and Gurkha officers sat at a long table, watching the men being entertained by the dancers and drinking rum.

Whenever a glass was half-empty there would be a cry of 'Raksi le' by a VCO, whereupon a full replacement would appear. With the rum and the beating of the *madals*, the party soon warms up until a Maruni approaches one of the junior officers, seductively inviting him to join in the dance. If he refuses, then a couple of smiling 'girls' forcibly drag him on to the impromptu stage, whereupon the standard of dancing deteriorates as the air of hilarity increases. Towards midnight the volume of music fades because the time has come for a goat to be sacrificed to Durga under the supervision of the *bahun*. Little time is wasted: the *bahun* mutters a prayer before sprinkling the ground, the executioner, and his victim, the goat, with holy water. For a moment there is silence while the executioner slowly raises his kukri in both hands, then brings the broad blade down. The head has come off cleanly in one blow; the choir bursts into a Hindu hymn, blank rounds are fired into the night sky and everyone laughs and hugs his neighbour. The battalion will have good fortune in battle and in all its other activities during the ensuing year: no one is ashamed of the superstitious happiness they feel. Then it is back to the party.

For the British officers and most of the revellers there is little sleep. After consuming large quantities of rum, the hangover and thirst that follow cannot be assuaged by drinking quantities of water—indeed to do so invites trouble as the rum reacts immediately. A traditional breakfast in the mess after a night of celebration would be extremely hot, peppery mulligatawny soup with bowls of rice and fresh lemon, followed by chicken and bacon fritters. After breakfast and fortified by one or two brandy and ginger ales, the officers then face the spectacle of Mar, with the whole battalion gathered round the sacrificial post. It is now time for the buffalo-headed demon, Mahishashura, to be sacrificed. A buffalo has been chosen to represent the demon and a man specially selected to perform the act of sacrifice. He carries a heavy sacrificial kukri, much larger than the service weapon and wielded with both hands. In one corner of the square the Gurkha wives and children are sitting as in an enormous flower bed, wearing saris like petals of every conceivable colour. At Mar, the animal is being offered in the name of the battalion and for the prayers to be answered it must be decapitated with one clean sweep of the kukri. Failure in this means that the prayers are not accepted and misfortune will dog the unit.

Not surprisingly, there is a hush of anxious expectancy as the kukri is raised and brought swiftly down. With one stroke the head is severed, the silence is broken by loud cheers, the blowing of bugles and banging of *madals*. The executioner, usually a powerfully-built man, then comes to stand before the commanding officer of the battalion who ties a white turban round his head as a public act of congratulation.

Then, in quick succession further sacrifices follow, each made on behalf of the different companies: there is the heavy smell of death in the air but among the men there is a sense of content and wellbeing if the heads have fallen as they should. The party spirit returns, the rejoicing is taken up, the rum flows again until, on the tenth day of the festival, the men receive the holy mark of Tika on their foreheads. Dashera is over for another year.

Nowadays there will be several differences, some superficial, others more important. For a start the Gurkha soldiers will not be wearing starched white shirts and shorts or sporting shaven heads and *tupis* under regimental side hats. In place of rum, the guests are offered a wide selection of alcoholic and soft drinks. The traditionalist will find in the long Dashera 'drama' that certain items and dances have not changed over the years. Comics still perform their acts of mimicry which can be amusing, shrewd and sometimes cruel. At the same time, there are likely to be Nepali and Hindu 'pop' tunes and possibly versions of popular Western dances. The dress of the Marunis, although still extremely feminine, reflect today's more sophisticated styles. The stage and its props are elaborate as are the lighting and musical instruments. The guest lists, too, often contain the names of those the unit wishes to thank for services rendered. The informal nautch of years gone by has been replaced by something more akin to a variety performance. On the debit side, it is a sad fact that dozens of Gurkha riflemen have to be employed on numerous fatigues, including acting as orderlies, instead of relaxing and enjoying their own festival.

All is not lost, however, because the author has been reassured by more than one of today's Commanding Officers that the trend for bigger and better 'drama' parties is being checked and, in certain instances, even reversed. The problem they have is to convince their Gurkha Major and his QGOs that the unit is not losing 'face' by reverting to the informal nautch, or even allowing each company to organize its own party so that the maximum number of men can join in the celebrations.

Another aspect that has had to be watched in recent times is the sacrificial killing of the buffalo which, inevitably, excites interest and can attract adverse comment. Recognizing the sensitivity of the issue—especially when the RSPCA and Anti-Blood Sports League are close at hand—the Gurkha battalion serving in the UK has never carried out this ceremony. Instead, the Training Depot in Hong Kong act as proxy by carrying out the sacrifice on behalf of the UK-based battalion. It is also noticeable that many of the modern-day Gurkha soldiers do not take such an active interest in the Mar ceremony, either because they do not believe in its religious aspects or, being far better educated than their predecessors, appreciate that it is a bloodthirsty performance and are slightly embarrassed about the public sacrifice.

One thing that has not changed over the years occurs when thick heads and increasing waistlines are hammered into shape during a battalion route march, organized on the first working day after the week-long festivities have drawn to a close.

The Nepali calendar contains so many festivals and holidays that the British Army has had to insist on only the most important ones being observed by the Brigade of Gurkhas. That notwithstanding, higher headquarters and neighbouring British units express amazement, combined with mock horror, at the number of holidays observed by their Gurkha friends—there is a degree of envy in their comments as well.

The last of the annual festivals is Tewar, known in India as Dewali, which takes place in October or November. This colourful festival lasts for five days and each day has a special name and a special object of worship. In chronological order these are: the crow, the dog, the cow, the ox and the brother. On the evening of the third day, special prayers are offered to Lachmi, Goddess of Wealth, and groups of children visit neighbouring houses to receive gifts. The next evening, when special favours are paid to oxen, parties go from house to house singing, following which their hosts offer them food and drink and the *madals* keep beating out their repetitive throbbing harmony until morning breaks.

The most important day of the festival is the last one, Bhai Tewar, and on this day every man must visit his sister. Naturally, there are many who have no blood sisters, in which case the man must find an adopted or god-sister who will perform the Bhai Tika ceremony. It is an elaborate procedure, too elaborate to describe here in detail, which ends with her anointing his head with oil and breaking a walnut, thus invoking a special magic against his enemies. The sister, or adopted sister, puts a little water into bowls of coloured powder and after mixing them into a separate paste, she affixes tikas (caste marks) on to her brother's forehead. Her blessing ends this rather moving ceremony and that night every house is decorated from courtyard to rooftop with many small lights, a beautiful sight. Even the dingy shanty town, Chowk Bazaar, in Darjeeling is transformed by the fairy lights into a place of beauty.

Although he was a keen and inveterate gambler himself, the great Jangbahadur Rana was the ruler who forbade gambling throughout Nepal, except during the festival of Tewar. This custom has continued and the annual sport starts on the beat of a drum. All else is thrown aside while the whole population gives itself up to the greatest passion of Nepal. And so it is in the Army, although, once again, there are quite a number of modern Gurkha soldiers who appear to take little interest in the gambling organized by their Gurkha Major within the unit lines. In years gone by, the majority threw themselves into the gambling without inhibition; the hoarse excited cries seemed far removed from the Gurkha soldier's normal disciplined behaviour. Many stories are told by the old soldiers about fortunes lost and won in their villages during Dewali, with animals, livestock, complete farms and even wives being won and lost on the throw of a dice. In today's Brigade of Gurkhas, strict control is exercised, the sale and drinking of alcohol being confined to certain hours and always under supervision.

So much for the festivals; now for a few items of folk lore. The average Gurkha soldier may laugh at witches, wizards and spirits, especially when talking to one of his British officers, but in reality many still retain a strong belief in the numerous creatures of their mythology. The ordinary wizard is known as Bokso and a witch as Boksi. In days gone by those suspected of witchcraft were occasionally beaten to death, and the exorcising of evil spirits is still practised— which includes the unit lines, especially when a soldier, a wife or child refuses to respond to Western-style medicine and behaves in an odd manner. A man who has been bewitched will sometimes fall to the ground insensible and if this happens he can only be saved with difficulty by five men, four of them grasping his thumbs and big toes, and the fifth the *tupi* on his head (or where one would be if he had one!). Ground chillis are put in his mouth and nose and a heated piece of metal is placed against his skin. This, the believers say, will produce burns not on him but on the wicked witch which has been tormenting his soul.

Witches often cast their spell on young children, whereupon the parents must carry out a special ceremony in accordance with the advice given by the professional exorcist. Generally speaking, this will involve a sacrifice of some sort or other, often a cockerel or hen. Those claiming to be able to exorcise evil spirits keep their powers secret and only pass them on to those of their children who seem especially receptive. The exorcist, who is usually a man, is paid for his services, which invariably means him going into a trance before he intonates incantations in a falsetto voice. The exorcists' dress varies depending on the type of ceremony involved; masks are often worn, although sometimes the exorcist conceals his face by blackening it.

After a death it is customary for the home to be ceremonially purified. Burning paper or jets of kerosene are sometimes used to burn the air inside the house and gongs and tin cans are beaten, conches blown and much shouting adds to the noise, all intended to frighten the dead man's spirit and drive it outside. In addition, it is common practice for a bamboo framework to be made, around which is wound a complicated maze of strings, forming symmetrical patterns. Into this is placed an effigy made of dough, money, flowers, coloured paper and rags, all of which represent the evil spirit. With a small offering of food, the cage is then taken from the house and placed near a crossroads. This is done to confuse the evil spirit so that it is unable to find its way back to the house and is thus banished for ever.

The Gurkhas have many superstitious beliefs, some of them centred round the snake. For example, to see a snake eating its prey is meant to be a sign that a close relative is about to die. If someone, on emerging from a house, sees a snake crossing the path, it means that there will be a severe illness in that home at some future date. If snakes are spotted by Gurkhas, they are usually attacked with vicious determination, perhaps because one of their beliefs is that even a decapitated snake can aim its head and inflict a fatal bite. Some Nepalese also believe that a snake that has been killed retains the poison in its tail for some time, which perhaps explains why many hillmen will continue beating the body of a dead snake until it is an unrecognizable mess.

Turning from animals to human beings, it is inauspicious to carry out marriage ceremonies between July and the end of August, the Nepalese month of Sawan. It is also inauspicious to leave home for a journey on a Saturday or to arrive back on a Tuesday. To get around the first canon, the pragmatic Gurkhas cope with a journey on a Saturday by making a short trip on the day before, when they deposit an article at a friend's house in the direction of the proposed journey. Then, next day, the journey technically starts after collecting the article from the friend's house. In such a way the gods have not been defied and the traveller can depart with an easy conscience!

Superstition states that clothes bought on a Monday should be burnt. If, however, this is the only available shopping day, the rule can be sidestepped by pulling a piece of fluff from the garment and casting it on the fire; in such a way is the superstition honoured and good fortune guaranteed. Eight is considered an unlucky number for a party and, if inviting guests, three kinds of meat should not be cooked together. Khorsani (chilli) should not be offered to a guest by hand; to do so is to invite a quarrel. A man seen in white clothes in a dream portends a death. Strangely enough, dreams of beating mean sickness while dreams of sickness promise health and happiness.

These are but a handful of the beliefs that are held even to this day in many of the remoter villages in the hills of Nepal. Strange maybe, but a Gurkha soldier serving in the UK wonders why his host throws salt over his left shoulder, or refuses to walk under a ladder, while his hostess worries about thirteen sitting down at table. He cannot understand why a black cat should bring luck because in his own country to be startled by a cat is considered an ill-omen and may well prove fatal!

But whereas the majority of British people tend to treat their superstitions lightly, many Gurkhas still revert to folk lore when they are sick, injured or faced with ill-fortune. A surprisingly large number of wounded Gurkha soldiers in wars gone by did not recover because they gave up the struggle mentally, often for reasons difficult for a Westerner to understand. Likewise, there have been several cases of Gurkha soldiers believing that they were under a spell, their health deteriorating rapidly for no apparent medical reason.

A strange incident involving Gurkha soldiers believing something outside the average Westerner's ken occurred during 1945 when a battalion of the 1st Gurkha Rifles was doing some jungle warfare training near Bangalore in South India. While one company was practising a river crossing, there was a shout of '*Manchhe dubyo*' ('a man has gone under'). He had sunk in about fifteen feet of water and an officer, John Rennie, after diving several times, located him and brought him to the surface. At least five minutes had elapsed between the time the man had sunk and the time his rescuers got him ashore. Rennie had a good knowledge of life-saving and started vigorous artificial respiration on the soldier. Although the Gurkhas around him were saying, 'Leave him alone, Sahib; he is dead', the officer disregarded their comments and continued working on the apparently lifeless body.

After about ten minutes the 'corpse' started breathing, to the astonishment of the bystanders. After all the water had been pumped out of him, he threw up, then sat up and stared around him, the whites of his eyes now bright red. John Rennie sent him to the Battalion First Aid Post and forgot about the whole matter until the company returned to base camp some days later. He was standing by himself in the jungle when suddenly the same Rifleman, Churamani Rana, appeared and said that he really was dead and that his bequest was that all his belongings including his wife, his child, his cow and other oddments, should go to Rennie. Later the surprised officer noticed that in the company the other men never spoke to Churamani directly and always used the past tense when mentioning him.

A few months later the Battalion went into action for the first time in Burma and, following a skirmish, Rennie asked what casualties the company had suffered, to be told that two men had been killed. Later that day he saw some Gurkhas pushing a captured Jap handcart down the road with a blanket over it and, on asking what was under the blanket, he was told that it covered the two dead men killed in the fighting during the morning. Rennie pulled the blanket back and three bodies were revealed. In surprise, he asked: 'What is going on? Why did you say that two men were killed when there are three bodies on the cart?'

'Oh, that one is Churamani but we didn't count him because he was drowned in the river crossing a few months ago.'

John Rennie's recollection is that, after nearly drowning in the river, Churamani acted as though he was a zombie and apparently never spoke another word, except his brief announcement of his last 'will' to his Sahib. Rennie had no explanation whatever of the other men's attitude towards Churamani but presumed that they had never seen artificial respiration before and as a consequence could not accept it as a fact, though drowning in Nepal was a fairly common death among Gurkhas, especially in the monsoon season. As a footnote to this strange story, John Rennie was awarded a Royal Humane Society's Certificate and the citation read: 'Which is hereby awarded him for having on the 7th January, 1945, gone to the rescue of a man who was in imminent danger of drowning in the Bhadra River, Southern India, and whose life he gallantly saved.'

But *did* he save Rifleman Churamani Rana's life?

Witch doctors (called *Jhakri* by the hill tribes) still play a big part in the lives of the peasant folk of Nepal. Even Gurkha officers, well educated, intelligent and outwardly Westernized, at times of crisis may consult a witch doctor rather than the British Medical Officer. Some Nepalese only go to see a doctor when the sacrifices to the gods have failed, but unfortunately by then it is often too late for Western medicine to succeed.

The witch doctors' cures are based on animals and the local vegetation, and some of their methods are pretty repulsive. An RAMC doctor commented: 'The victims must either possess blind faith or be temporarily unbalanced even to accept such treatment!' Every disease has its own treatment and usually it is the more revolting ones which are inflicted on the simple villagers by these witch doctors.

In a country where snake bites are common, severe burns to children from spluttering fat caused by open-fire cooking are sadly prevalent, and diseases which have been tamed in the Western world still claim countless victims each year, the witch doctors will continue to practise their form of magic for many years to come. Tuberculosis remains the most terrible scourge in Nepal because TB treatment— costing between £25 and £50—is far too expensive for the majority of the Nepalese. So to the witch doctors they go. The witch doctors could not have chosen a more diseased animal than the jackal to cure such a debilitating disease for, incredible as it may seem, it is jackal's meat that is given to TB sufferers.

TB, cholera and many other diseases mean that the life expectancy in Nepal is still twenty to twenty-five years below that in the UK. The medical problems are countless in a country where the standard of living is so low and where the hard-working peasants face sufferings beyond the comprehension of our Western world.

Against such a background, is it surprising that witch doctors exert so much influence and superstitions play such a big part in the lives of the country folk?

NINE

Nepal—Yesterday
and Today

At the end of the Second World War Britain's staunch friend, the Maharajah Judha, retired to India to live a life of contemplation; in some luxury, it must be said, as he took with him his vast wealth and the strippings of the Treasury. He was succeeded by his nephew, Padma Shamsher, whose authority was soon to be undermined by the impending withdrawal of the British from the Indian subcontinent. To the British negotiators Nepal mattered little in the scheme of things, although they expressed the pious hope that India would not meddle in the internal affairs of her tiny neighbour. At first, and certainly in public, the Indian Government under Pandit Nehru maintained a friendly and correct attitude to the neighbouring kingdom, although both countries realized that land-locked Nepal was completely dependent on India for the free transit of goods.

Although Nepal remained in virtual isolation from world forces until the end of the 1940s, the country's rulers had seen portents of the future and were taking belated steps to liberalize their régime. In 1948 the Constitution Act was promulgated by the Maharajah which envisaged a form of government such as India had in the 1920s, with a legislature and council of ministers consisting of a mixture of nominated and elected members. These latter were to be returned by a system of indirect election, based primarily upon village and town *panchayats*, or councils of elders. But in the eyes of his fellow Ranas, Padma was moving too fast; they pointed out that out in the hills, life went on as usual as it does to this day in many respects. The peasants tilled their fields, and built new houses when the priest condemned the old ones as being ill-omened. The majority of the simple hillmen were not persuaded of the blessings of self-government and showed little enthusiasm for exercising their franchise, still less for standing for election.

In April, 1948, it was the turn of Maharajah Padma Shamsher to retire voluntarily; he realized that he was not strong enough to cope with affairs and was succeeded by his cousin, Mohan Shamsher, who introduced the new Constitution which Padma had promised the country. Political agitation in Kathmandu contrived to keep the Valley in turmoil; the police had to be used on several occasions to break up gatherings and decrees were issued banning the pro-Congress Party, as well as imposing a stringent censorship on the Press. The Congress Party, after some few hundred of its members were arrested, moved away from Kathmandu to Raxaul, over the border in India, from where it launched a non-violent campaign to secure political rights. In Kathmandu the quarrel between the King—who up to then had been a figurehead like his predecessors—and the Maharajah was exploited by ambitious politicians. The Press in India was consistently and violently opposed to the Rana régime, and actively supported the Indian Congress and Nepalese National Congress Parties which displayed hostility to that family. Preparations for 'invasions' from Indian soil began at the same time as Maharajah Mohan was negotiating a treaty of friendship with India which stipulated that there would be everlasting peace and friendship between the Governments of India and Nepal. Mohan warned India that an invasion of his country was being prepared from their soil and his information was well-founded. Towards the end of 1950 the Nepal border was crossed at nine points by the forces of the Indian-inspired Nepal Congress Party and a few days later Pandit Nehru admitted that his government wanted progressive democracy in Nepal, adding that he officially recognized King Tribhuvana as the supreme authority in that land.

Surprisingly, perhaps, in the Valley of Nepal there was no responsive uprising, while in the Western hills the villagers remained unruffled. In the East—where the quicker-tempered Limbus and Rais live—there were widespread outbreaks of violence and within a few weeks many of the main centres in East Nepal had been taken over by rebel forces. The King took matters into his own hands in February, 1951, by proclaiming the termination of the hereditary premiership and transferring most of the Maharajah's powers to himself. Chaos persisted in the Valley; there was no progress because the new rulers had no conception of how to administer, how to plan or how to govern. Inevitably the Ranas and Congress members fell out and it was not surprising that students took matters into their own hands and riots led to one or two deaths. In December, 1951, Maharajah Mohan Shamsher, now over 70, retired to live at Bangalore in South India: his departure marked the end of Gurkha supremacy in Nepal and heralded the final twilight of the Ranas.

Thereafter the political situation became even more complicated as parties within parties intrigued against each other. In May, 1956, the King, Mahendra Bir Bikram Shah, was crowned in Kathmandu and six years later he introduced a partyless, tiered *panchayat* democracy which provided for councils at village, district, zonal and national levels. However, only the village councils were directly chosen by the people, the rest were indirectly elected so that, in effect, it was a one-party system with all major policies being decided by the King. He hired and fired prime ministers at will. At least his system had the advantage of stopping the quarrelling among the politicians, but it allowed virtually no political expression as only persons who actively supported the *panchayat* system were allowed to stand for election. Moreover, it was inefficient, since all the power resided in the King, so that his subordinates were reluctant to take decisions, even on comparatively minor matters. In places it was corrupt, with local *panchayats* working the system to their own advantage. Its worst feature was that those who made the policy did not have to submit to the verdict of the ballot box every few years and no one was encouraged to offer alternative solutions to those that had been approved by the King.

King Mahendra died in January, 1972, and was succeeded by his son, the young King Birendra Bir Bikran Shah Dev. Like his father, the new King affirmed his belief, 'that a political system suitable to Nepalese conditions had been well established and [his] Government would turn its efforts towards improving the standard of living of his people within the existing political system'. Brave words but beneath the surface there were undercurrents which could not be suppressed for ever.

By the spring of 1979 popular discontent with corrupt officials, steeply rising prices and inadequate supplies of basic necessities reached a climax. In April of that year students went to the Pakistan Embassy to demonstrate against the execution of Bhutto, the deposed President of Pakistan, and were roughly handled by the police. From then on there were strikes and demonstrations by students throughout

Nepal, demanding democratic rights and an end to the then current 'anti-people government'. There were many scuffles between students and police and a few days later some groups of workers joined the students in a few demonstrations. At the end of May there was quite a serious disturbance in Kathmandu when government buildings were set on fire and the police lost control of the situation until order was restored by the Army—although in only about a platoon's strength.

That was enough to spark the King into action and, speaking on Radio Nepal, he announced that there would be a nationwide referendum to determine whether the citizens of Nepal wished to continue the existing system of government, under which party politics were forbidden, or to replace it with a multi-party system. Although he kept out of the subsequent public debate, the King had always claimed that a party system would lead to a country divided on ethnic grounds, and there is much evidence to support that statement. The referendum took place a year later in May and the result was a 55 per cent vote in favour of the existing *panchayat* system. In general the towns voted for a party political system, while in the rural areas the vote went clearly in favour of the *panchayats*. The King had declared that, whichever side won the referendum, the National Legislature would be directly chosen by the electorate and, of even greater importance, the Prime Minister would be elected in that way as well.

The King adhered to his promise and the National Constitution was duly amended and in May, 1981, the first general election was held under the partyless system. It must be added that the King still retains the right to nominate one-fifth of the members of the Legislature, and his retention of ultimate authority surprises visitors because in public he presents a pleasant but far from strong image, showing little enthusiasm for any event he is watching or attending in an official capacity. However, he is regarded by many of his people as a reincarnation of Vishnu and this fact alone ensures strong support for him, particularly in the mountain villages. At the time of writing Nepal continues to be a strong monarchy in which the King rules the people directly, all major decisions still coming from the Palace. His opponents maintain that little has changed since his father's death but this allegation is not wholly borne out by the facts.

Nepal is now open to the world. Tourism brings in some £25,000,000 annually, against which figure must be set the fact that some two-thirds of that sum is spent on importing luxury goods, foods and other items required to support the tourist industry. Great strides have been made in education and in communications, the two major factors which had helped to keep the country in the dark ages in the past. Foreign aid has poured in from donor countries and international organizations and is by far the greatest source of foreign currency for Nepal, running at about £160,000,000 per year. Nepal is a staunch member of the non-aligned group in the United Nations and is at pains to be friendly with everyone, but inevitably her greatest preoccupation must be with her giant neighbours, India and China. Her policy is one of equidistance, to be on good terms with both, although on several occasions since the Second World War, relations with India have not been smooth, chiefly because there has been a tendency on the Government of India's part to play the big brother and wield a heavy stick. When India absorbed the small state of Sikkim, the Nepalese were greatly alarmed, and relations were cool for several months thereafter. Nepal's landlocked position means that overland imports and exports have to pass through India, so that country is always in a position to strangle Nepal economically; this hard fact of life does not help to establish a cordial relationship.

In contrast, feelings towards China are warm, possibly because she is seen as a counterweight to India, and there have been few disagreements between the two countries. The King visited Peking in 1979. Perhaps it would be fair to say that both China and India are content to have Nepal as a buffer between them, provided she does not lean too far in one direction or the other. One thing is certain; the fact that the country has continued to maintain its independence is largely due to the King and his father before him; both have walked the delicate tightrope with great skill.

Outside the world of politics Nepal has other problems to resolve. In 1958 her population was just under 8½ million; in the 1981 National Census it had reached over 15 million. It is not surprising that, with improved communications, there has been a mass exodus from the hills down to the Kathmandu Valley, to Pokhara in the West, and to the Terai Plain. Whereas in 1954, 71 per cent of the population were living in the hill regions, now it is about 50 per cent. Many of the shanty towns in the Terai are so dirty, dilapidated and unhygienic that at first it is difficult to understand why so many people have abandoned the tidy mountain villages and the cool clean air. The icy water from sparkling mountain springs can taste like nectar but in so many of the villages, precious loads of water have to be carried in pitchers and buckets up to the houses—just one of the many tiresome chores that the women have to perform throughout the year. It is not surprising that drinking water so carried is basically used for cooking and drinking and that there is little to spare for washing or other luxuries.

To a visitor, life in a picturesque hill village appears to be an idyllic existence and, in a way, it can be so for the young, the strong and the able-bodied. The picture changes when there is an accident, serious illness or when a natural disaster strikes—as it often does when the monsoon deluge causes landslides and turns rivers into raging torrents. In most parts of the hills there are no hospitals so that the sick and injured have to be carried over rough tracks, often for days on end, in a basket strapped to the back of a sturdy relative, friend or neighbour. After such a hazardous journey, they arrive at one of the few district hospitals which are well below the standard of their equivalent in the United Kingdom. It becomes a question of the survival of the fittest. Life in the hills is no fun for the senile, infirm or badly disabled, though these unfortunates are given as much help as possible by relatives and neighbours. The aged are listened to with respect and there is no sending 'granny' away to an old folks' home as so often happens in the West.

So it is not altogether surprising that many hill people turn their backs on their old homes to seek easier conditions down in the Terai or in Kathmandu. Instead of back-breaking climbs for the women with heavy loads of water and firewood, piped water of a sort is usually available in the shanty towns and on the plains. The children can go to school by bus instead of meandering over mountain tracks, often walking up to two hours each way. The surroundings may be more sordid but life generally is easier—especially for the women. Moreover, there are a handful of hospitals which can be reached by bus or taxi instead of the sick being carried by a porter on journeys which during the rains can be dangerous and frightening.

The King and his Government have been trying to control the ever-increasing exodus from the hills and in the past have cracked down on illegal squatters who tried to settle in parts of the Terai forests—not always using minimum force. Some Government officials in Kathmandu have expressed the hope that after the hill centres have been linked by road, then the standard of living in the interior will rise and the people will no longer desert their villages for the settlements on the plains. This may prove to be a pious hope, as it did when the English set out to pacify the Highlands of Scotland. After the English built roads into the Highlands, it heralded a steady exodus of the clans which eventually speeded up until today the hills and glens are left to the sheep in the winter and the tourists in the summer. The Nepalese highlands may not be similarly depopulated but the expensive roads being constructed by foreign countries—India, China, USA and the UK—undoubtedly will speed up the exodus rather than inducing the hill tribes to stay put. Whether the Brigade of Gurkhas likes it or not, each year that passes will make it more and more difficult to enlist young boys who have genuinely been brought up in the hill villages of their ancestors—although they may claim a close acquaintance in order to be enrolled!

It is, perhaps, an opportune moment to assess how Great Britain has attempted to repay the considerable debt she owes to her staunch ally, Nepal. The Brigade of Gurkhas, with a current strength of some 8,500 officers and men, directly or indirectly brings some £15m into the country each year. That sum includes remittances of pay from serving soldiers to relatives; pensions; pay of locally employed civilians and works projects sponsored by PSA; and the Royal Nepal Air Lines Corporation's 'Gurkha Air Lift' contract which moves some 14,000 passengers each year, not only within the country itself but to and from Hong Kong. Indeed, the Brigade is by far Royal Nepal Airline's most lucrative customer. And by having three fairly large military establishments on Nepalese soil, British-inspired local purchases and contracts also help the surrounding community to a marked degree.

At a great cost, Great Britain has constructed a road which runs from Biratnagar in the Eastern Terai through the town of Dharan and then up and over the giant Tamar River, before climbing rapidly to Dhankutta, one of the main centres in East Nepal. Along the Terai runs the recently completed East-West Highway, parts of which have been constructed by four nations, the British building a part in West Nepal.

Currently the Royal Nepalese Army is receiving generous support from the UK in terms of overseas training and equipment (including a £2m 'gift' package). Some might say that this assistance has been given tardily, but the timing of such aid has had to be carefully considered, especially in a capital like Kathmandu where embassies from both sides of the Iron Curtain watch each move that is made.

Every gift given is analysed by friend and foe alike, so nothing must be done which could cause embarrassment to the Nepalese Government.

Compared with the roads and other expensive aid projects, the small British Military Hospital at Dharan, in East Nepal, may be a poor relation but for the benefits it brings to a wide area the hospital must be placed near the top of the list. The BMH was first established to cover the needs of the serving soldiers, their dependents, and the British Army Gurkha pensioners living in East Nepal. As the years have passed, however, the official patients have become but a fraction of the workload carried out in the 80-bed hospital. People of all ages walk, or are carried, for miles to attend 'villagers' clinics' which are held at regular intervals. For the British staff it is rewarding work of great professional interest because they have to treat a range of diseases and illnesses rarely, if ever, encountered in their own country. It can also be heartrending because there are never enough beds, never enough hours for operations, never enough time to diagnose and treat so many people. Over the years the BMH has established an enviable reputation and has won more friends than any other British-sponsored project in Nepal. With an eye to the long-term, constructive steps have been taken to train Nepali technicians, nurses and other staff against the day when the British leave. It is then hoped that Nepali staff will be able to carry on in the same way as their RAMC counterparts have done over the last twenty years.

The Gurkha Welfare Appeal is something that is little known outside the Brigade of Gurkhas and a comparatively small circle of friends and loyal supporters. As stated before, the Appeal was the brainchild of Major-General Patterson who, as MGBG, had the melancholy task of organizing the run-down after the Confrontation in Borneo had ended. The purpose of the Appeal was to help the large numbers of ex-soldiers who had to be returned to Nepal with small pensions or with no pension at all. Some distinguished men in the UK headed the Appeal, with Field-Marshal Lord Harding as Chairman. Its aim was to assist all ex-servicemen, and their dependents, who had served the British Crown at any time, in war or in peace. Donations were sought from many parts of the world, but, in retrospect, it is clear that the important decision first to raise as much money as possible by self-help, harnessing the talents of officers and men still serving with the Brigade, paid dividends, because such a gesture showed the world that the Brigade itself was taking active steps to meet the challenge. There were numerous 'fun fairs' and other functions organized by the officers and men which attracted large crowds ready to spend money generously as well as enjoying themselves. After the original target of £1,000,000 had been reached, the Appeal continued to build up reserves so that the income from the money, wisely invested, continues to be sufficient to meet the ever-rising costs in Nepal—but only just. There are no grounds for complacency and the commitment is unlikely to get less as time goes by.

Raising the money was just the start of the process: ensuring that it got to the right people was much more difficult, especially in areas lacking communications, banks and other facilities that we take for granted. Over the years an organization has been established which now covers most parts of the traditional recruiting areas in East and West Nepal. At twenty-four Welfare Centres—the number can vary slightly from year to year—retired Gurkha officers act as Area Welfare Officers (AWOs), responsible for all the ex-servicemen and their dependents living within those districts. To assist the AWOs, there are medically trained assistants, usually pensioner warrant officers or senior NCOs, who have successfully undergone a 9-month course sponsored and run under British aid. In a few centres there are also agricultural assistants, similarly trained under the auspices of the FCO, who are there to pass on their knowledge and expertise to the local people, advising them about their crops and demonstrating better methods of looking after their livestock.

When disaster strikes, the breadwinner dies, or a landslide takes away the livelihood of an ex-serviceman, the case is investigated by the AWO who is empowered to give a small sum of money on the spot to meet immediate needs. If major assistance is considered necessary, then the applicant is sent down to one of the two British Gurkha Depots where, after a thorough investigation, financial help of a more long-term nature can be given in the form of a one-time grant or, possibly, a small welfare pension. Certain changes and refinements have been made as a result of experience and the whole organization is reviewed each year. For example, instead of renting indifferent houses, as was done at first, the Welfare Centres are now being purpose-built and are owned by the Trust so that there is an air of permanency about most of the Centres which reflect a reasonably high standard of cleanliness and hygiene to serve as an example to the hill folk who continue to be backward in both these aspects—

including, it must be admitted, many lethargic ex-servicemen who revert to their earlier habits in a distressingly short time.

In certain parts of the hills, the Gurkha Welfare Trust and its associated projects, some of which have been generously funded by the Canadian Government, have improved the lot of several villages and their inhabitants. Water pumps, irrigation projects, footbridges, improvements to schools or even in one or two places the actual construction of the school buildings: the list covers a wide range of projects and is invariably challenging. (For more detail and statistics, see Appendix B.)

We have seen that Nepal is changing, although the traditionalists might argue that many things are being done too quickly and certainly in recent years Kathmandu and Pokhara have changed out of all recognition. In 1947 the sole foreigners in the Valley were the British; now there are seventy-five nations with accredited diplomatic links, of whom nineteen have resident missions in Kathmandu, while there is a plethora of organizations such as UNESCO, the Peace Corps and Voluntary Service Organization, to name but three. Each year an ever-increasing influx of tourists descend on the country. Deforestation and soil erosion are driving many villagers down to the dusty heat of the Terai, the better to provide for their families, and inevitably the traditions of their clans, including the influence of their elders, are weakened by these moves.

Honorary Lieutenant Harikanta Rai, a pensioner from the 10th Gurkhas, was one of those officers who settled in the Terai, for reasons he describes:

A soldier after retirement invariably chooses to settle in an area near the town mainly because of the children's education. It also allows his wife and children to adapt to the local system gradually and without depriving them straightaway of electricity, water and other amenities.

Whether the migrants down on the plains are really well off is a debatable point. One British officer who has spent many years in Nepal, both as a serving officer and as a civilian, feels that the proportion of ex-servicemen who die before their due time is much higher down on the plains than among those who have remained in their hill villages. While it would be difficult, if not impossible, to prove this, other officers in the Brigade tend to agree.

The present-day soldier's attitude to life and his eventual retirement has undoubtedly changed for the better. In Lieutenant Harikanta's words:

> Until the late 1960s leave men's main pastime was to go singsonging, drinking and getting involved with women at Dhan Nautch (Limbu dance) and Dhol Nautch (dance performed by a line of drummers). A number of them were to be seen reporting back at the Depot, at their own request, several weeks ahead of their actual reporting dates and totally bankrupt. Many of them fell prey to local loan-sharks borrowing money on condition that they would pay back sending gold from Malaya and Hong Kong ... One will not see those kind these days.

Certainly a change for the better! The soldier of the 1980s is more cautious about his future. He has travelled a great deal and so his outlook is much broader: he calculates his future. Harikanta comments:

> He has been in the UK much longer than his predecessors and so he has seen the life system of people in England more closely. He knows how, when and where to invest money and so he is prepared to face retired life a little bit more comfortably. This is where the lives of the 'old' and 'new' pensioners differ.

While not disagreeing with Harikanta's views, it would be wrong to give a sweeping and inaccurate impression that all who leave the Army do so with a tidy nest egg. For a start the ex-soldier's income drops some 75 per cent when he retires on a pension. Employment in the Terai is difficult, so those who do not own enough property face considerable problems. In these cases it would certainly be better if the men concerned returned to their old homes in the hills and those that do generally appear to reintegrate into the old community life and are happy. Lieutenant Harikanta met such an ex-NCO from his own battalion, looking remarkably healthy and told him that, 'he was looking like a ripe tomato', whereupon the old NCO remarked: '*You* drink dirty water of Dharan and still table-borne; come up in hills and try fresh water and tongba [a local drink]. You will understand what a life is!'

Harikanta concluded that there were many like himself, 'who have to be in the Terai and for some time continue to take on the jobs they are able to come by for the family's well-being and the children's education in particular'. This last comment is the nub of the problem—the desire to give their children the best possible education, even if it means sacrificing their own health and in some cases dissipating their modest savings. Education is often regarded as the paramount criterion for success, but how few of them even know the sad truth that the spread of education does not necessarily mean the spread of happiness? Sadly, too, not a few of the children fail to understand how much their parents have done for them and, being superficially better educated, regard their elders as being ignorant and illiterate. This is in complete contrast to the natural courtesy shown by the young in the hill villages towards the elderly—so, let us hope that old customs will prevail, even in the Terai and Valley of Kathmandu.

TEN

The Sahib and the Man

Sahib is one who is infallible, the decision-maker, who likes red chillies with his bhat, and who is partially spastic on the volley ground.

Tongue in cheek, the writer pokes gentle fun at his British officer, well aware that many dislike eating red hot chillies with their *bhat* (curry), and while it would be easy to treat the sahibs' so-called infallibility in the same light as a piece of mild sarcasm, nevertheless it would be a misunderstanding of the man, the Gurkha, if we did so. The truth is simple: to explain it is far more difficult. I am indebted to Captain (now Major) Maniprasad Rai, one of the first Gurkhas to be commissioned at the Royal Military Academy, Sandhurst, for this rational explanation of his countrymen's allegiance to the British Crown.

This allegiance is one of the realities which cannot be explained away merely in terms of cold logic and the exactitude of modern materialism without introducing that old-fashioned friendship and trust between peoples who have, through a unique fellowship, in spite of the difference of race and colour, developed that kinship and independence on each other's abilities. Bonds between London and Kathmandu have been probably stronger than would have been the case had the British colonized Nepal. If this is true, then one must conclude that the bonds of the allegiance draws its strength from the very fact that no other bonds exist, particularly those that ring a political note.

Perceptive words and Major 'Mani' goes on to analyse a typical cheerful rifleman:

> He is Rfn Purnabahadur Rai. He is basically a simple, uneducated, hardworking cheerful soul who has little interest outside the satisfaction of having done his day's duties, having a Tiger beer or a coke at the NAAFI with his friends, reminiscing about his home, and events in his professional career ... He is a great respecter of his ancestors and early in life he learns that his father has an absolute authority in the family. This as a general rule leads to a great respect for elders and the aged, or, conversely, to treat his superiors as if they were his elders who are endowed with more experience, foresight and wisdom. Hence the reason why senior NCOs are referred to as 'Sargeant Ba' or 'Major (WOII) Ba' and Gurkha Officers' wives as 'Captain-Ni Ama'. For 'Ba' and 'Ama' mean father and mother, that is how it looks to our Rifleman Purnabahadur, and if as happens with Gurkha officers, age is combined with authority, the power is formidable indeed.

It would be difficult for any British officer, however experienced he might be as a result of service with the Brigade or domicile in Nepal, to reach the heart of the matter like Maniprasad has done. Witness a final assessment of the man contained in the same excellent account:

> His loyalty and obedience of particular orders are phenomenal—to the extent that justice could not be done to it in an article so short as this. Hence, one would be right in attributing a large share of the Gurkha's prowess in battle to this absolute obedience to orders and loyalty to his leader. Thus the man is laid bare for the analyst and admirers alike, the qualities which makes him feared as an adversary, loved as a person, respected by comrades in arms.

From the above we can understand why the British officer set in authority over him has a head start as far as the young Gurkha recruit is concerned: the sahib *is* his 'Sarkar' (government) while the man is serving and the fact that his officer is of a different race, colour and creed is immaterial and does not diminish in any way the Gurkha's respect for him.

The Gurkha soldier, with the benefit of the innate qualities that are his birthright, is also the product of selection and training. The selection of recruits has already been described. From the time he is selected and enlisted at the Recruiting Depot in Nepal to the time he joins his unit is almost a year. The major part of this year he spends at the Training Depot in the New Territories of Hong Kong, undergoing a rigorous course which turns him into the dedicated professional the world knows.

Hard though the training is, it is remembered with nostalgia. Even Gurkhas who have gone on to qualify for Sandhurst have been known to refer to their recruit days at the training depot as the happiest of their service.

Minor misdemeanours in the Brigade rarely, if ever, lead to the offender being marched before the Commanding Officer. Any QGO worth his salt will deal with the day-to-day offences without recourse to formal charges. How they do this so effectively is something that the wiser British Company Commanders accept with gratitude: if it works well, then 'don't delve any deeper' would be their advice. So the average Company Commander rarely has to administer justice, only being required to do so when his QGO feels that the offender deserves an official punishment or if he is a habitual miscreant.

No one is keen to see a charge recorded on a soldier's documents as there is far more stigma attached to an entry than in a British unit. For this reason the Company Commander has carefully to weigh up the gravity of the alleged crime, the effect an official punishment might have on the soldier's behaviour thereafter and his long-term promotion prospects, against the fact that an over-lenient punishment would smack of failure to support one of his Gurkha officers, who had taken the comparatively unusual step of marching the 'bad lad' in front of the sahib.

A retired Colonel tells a story about the honesty—and naivety—of two riflemen in his company, way back in 1936. The two men, who were being groomed for promotion to Lance Naik (Lance-Corporal), were brought before him for causing a disturbance in the lines after lights out, 'in that they were fighting'. The trial went something like this:

'Why were you fighting?'
'Sahib, we were gambling, playing cards for money and he' (pointing at the other man) 'cheated, so, of course, I hit him and we started to fight.'
There was consternation in the company commander's heart.

There was a Regimental Standing Order which stated that anyone found gambling went straight in front of the CO when the punishment would be 28 days' detention—without any option. If these young riflemen received such a punishment, then their promotion prospects would disappear for ever. So, carefully choosing his words, he said: 'As I understand it, you were just playing cards but not for money. Is that correct?' To which they both replied, 'No, Sahib, we really were gambling.'

The Company Commander thought hard before telling the Gurkha officer to march them out of the office. He then told the Platoon Commander that if the men persisted in saying they were gambling it was a matter for the Colonel. However, if it was just a question of playing cards and having a minor scuffle thereafter, then it was within his powers to deal with the offence. The Gurkha officer nodded, saluted and went out to talk to the miscreants.

Five minutes later they were marched back, both with broad smiles on their faces, to agree that they were merely playing cards and duly apologized for their bad behaviour. They received seven days' 'Line Kaid' (confined to barracks) and in due course became excellent NCOs.

Soft? Perhaps; but in ninety-nine cases out of a hundred such treatment has proved wholly effective and long may it so continue.

To ask any officer or ex-officer of the Brigade for his opinion of his beloved Gurkha is to invite paeans of praise, the reasons for which have been touched on already when we followed the recruit into the army, admired his prowess in war and his patience and good humour in peace. Now it is time to take a closer look at the sahibs, the British officers who command them.

Hailing from the same background and being together at the RMA Sandhurst, the British officers who join the Brigade on posting are no better or worse than their equivalent British service counterparts. However, after a subaltern has joined a Gurkha battalion, he finds that he has to adjust to a different style of leadership which might—and it would be wrong to be more adamant than that—change the young officer's personality imperceptibly over the years: for the better, would be the claim made by the officers in the Brigade!

Customs have changed, as have the uniforms and, to a large extent, the recreational pursuits, but the paternal style of leadership adopted in the early days of the Brigade persists to this day. Let us look at a few of the more illustrious officers of years gone by.

Starting with the Sirmoor Rifles' founder, Frederick Young, there has been an impressive line of British officers who have gained renown as soldiers. Charles Reid, the defender of Hindu Rao's House, ended his illustrious career as General Sir Charles. Thereafter, the number of officers who reached the rank of Major-General or above is impressively high. After asking the ten Regimental Association secretaries for details, any thought of publishing a list disappeared, so many names were received. All that can be said is that service with the old Indian Army Gurkha Brigade could not have diminished prospects of promotion. The total was forty but some historian may care to challenge that figure.

In the Victorian era only the British officers were eligible for the supreme award for valour, the VC, their Gurkha soldiers having to wait until the First World War before they could win it. Between the Indian Mutiny and the end of Queen Victoria's reign, eleven officers of the Brigade won the VC. During the Burma campaign between 1942 and 1945 two more young British officers were to win the award posthumously. Their names were Captain Michael Allmand of the 6th and Major Frank Blaker of the 9th Gurkha Rifles.

If a list of all the British officers who have ever won decorations for gallantry while serving with Gurkhas was compiled, it would show just how many leaders have inspired their men at times when courageous leadership was vital. The truth is that Gurkha soldiers—like any other soldiers in the world—can only be as good as the officers who lead them. When there is mutual admiration, trust and respect, then the resulting combination becomes formidable, verging on the unbeatable. Britain's Brigade of Gurkhas would lay claim to both those distinctions.

Lord Kitchener of Khartoum was perhaps the most distinguished officer ever to have had an official connection with the Gurkha Brigade. Although Kitchener was a Royal Engineer, the period he spent as Commander-in-Chief in India brought him into contact with Nepal and her Gurkha warriors and he became Colonel of the 7th Gurkha Rifles in 1908. He was to hold this honorary appointment until the day he died, 5 June, 1916, when the cruiser HMS *Hampshire*, which was taking him to Russia, was sunk in the North Sea.

During and just after the First World War, the doyen of the Brigade was Brigadier-General The Hon Charles Bruce who, in his time, knew more about the Himalayas and the Gurkhas than any other officer in the Brigade. Charles Bruce was a great character, a bouncy extrovert about whom many stories have been told, an officer who was much loved by the men. He was immensely strong and when he was CO, his Adjutant was asked by the Medical Officer, who was checking officers for 'active service' in 1914, 'How does the CO manage to keep up with the Battalion in the field?' He got the answer, as quoted from the MO's notes: 'Why, man, he can tire out any BO or GO in the Battalion on the longest field day and no one can beat him on a hill.'

In the Officers' Mess on Guest Nights he would pick up two officers by the scruff of the neck and hold them out at arm's length.

Early in 1922 Charles Bruce had occasion to see his doctor about a suspected heart murmur (a false alarm as it turned out). The specialist expressed satisfaction with his condition but asked him to come back in six months' time, adding that he should take it easy when going up long flights of stairs.

The six months duly passed and Charles Bruce went to see the specialist, looking the very picture of health.

'Good,' exclaimed the doctor, 'I see you've been following my advice, General; taking it easy and relaxing.'

'Yes,' replied Charles Bruce, who was then in his mid-fifties, 'at my age, I didn't think it wise to go above 24,000 feet.'

He had been leader of the 1922 Everest Expedition! His nephew, Geoffrey Bruce, was one of the lead climbers and reached over 27,000 feet on the same expedition; like Charles he was in the 6th Gurkhas and became a Major-General in the Second World War.

After Charles Bruce's retirement, he went out to the 6th Gurkha Regimental Centre at Abbotabad to celebrate his 70th birthday. After a drink or two he challenged the British and Gurkha officers present to race him up the *khud* racecourse. He was the first to the top where they all celebrated with beer before the old warrior raced them down again. Fluent in several Nepali dialects, it is no wonder that he was a legend in so many hill villages.

Several of the young officers who fought in the First World War and survived to serve on as regulars in peacetime were to become famous in the 1939/45 war. Field-Marshal Lord Slim had done most of his regimental soldiering with the 6th Gurkha Rifles, which included participation in the Gallipoli campaign, before taking command of the 2/7th Gurkha Rifles in 1938. Bill Slim and 14th Army,

'The Forgotten Army', became synonymous in the annals of the Second World War. He was a man who led an army from despair and disaster to final victory, who spent 3½ years in that campaign as a Corps or Army Commander at the very centre of activity—truly the architect of victory. Slim was a generous man, a modest one, who had a deep understanding of strategy at the highest level but remained a human person with a fund of anecdotes and stories about the officers and men who fought under his command. To have been in continuous command of a corps or army in action for so long speaks volumes for his robustness and his skill as a tactician. It is not surprising that he is regarded as one of the greatest commanders of the Second World War.

Bill Slim's sense of humour and humanity made him a popular figure, not only while he was serving in the Army but later when he became a much-loved Governor-General of Australia. When Queen Elizabeth and Prince Philip were touring there, before air travel had opened up the interior, the Royal cavalcade went across the great continent by train with the Governor-General in attendance. In the outback the train stopped as there was to be an official function in the late afternoon. Bill Slim, dressed in his full regalia, had a few minutes to spare before he went down to collect the Queen and the Duke, so he pushed back the swing doors of a bar, empty except for a barman.

The barman looking up from cleaning a glass and exclaimed: 'Jeesus Christ!'

Quick as a flash, the bemedalled apparition in white replied, 'No, Bill Slim—Governor-General.'

It was no wonder that the Aussies loved him.

Some of Slim's chief lieutenants as corps and divisional commanders were officers from the old Indian Army Gurkha Brigade: General Sir Geoffrey Scoones; Major-General W. D. A. Lentaigne (successor to Orde Wingate as Commander Special Forces, the 'Chindits'); Major-General D. T. (Punch) Cowan, surely the most experienced divisional commander in the Burma campaign; Major-General D. M. Murray-Lyon who was made scapegoat in Malaya in 1942; Major-General Bruce Scott; Major-General D. D. Gracey (later to be General Sir Douglas when he was C-in-C Pakistan); these and many other distinguished officers had learnt their trade as company and battalion commanders with Gurkha troops and served under the best of them all, Bill Slim.

In the Middle East campaign Lieutenant-General Sir Francis

(Gertie) Tuker earned himself a worldwide reputation as commander of the famous 4th Indian Division, a skilful tactician and leader, and only ill health prevented him reaching the top after the war. As a writer, his research into Nepalese history was to produce the classic *Gorkha*, which the Brigade still rely on for much of their knowledge of the pre-1950 era. Following Gertie Tuker, the next three commanders of the 4th Indian Division all came from the Gurkha Brigade: Major-Generals A. W. Holworthy, 'Os' Lovett and Sir Charles Boucher.

Prior to 1947, the Brigade could claim a galaxy of distinguished officers. After becoming an integral part of the British Army, promotion in peacetime has been slow, inevitably, but nine officers have reached Major-General's rank (up to 1983), usually when taking up a three-year appointment as MGBG, the highest post any serving officer can achieve within the Brigade. One who achieved further promotion was General Sir Walter Walker, whose masterly defence of the Borneo territories during the Confrontation with Sukarno's Indonesia won the day, even though he did not receive the recognition he so richly deserved at the time. He had to wait two or three years before he received a knighthood and became more widely known as the subject of an excellent book by Tom Pocock, *Fighting General*.

Suspecting that over the years the Brigade officers have boasted a variety of talents—apart from the martial ones—the Regimental Association secretaries were asked to send in names of those who have achieved a measure of fame in other fields.

From the replies received, the final roll call looks like this:

Governor General of New Zealand and Marshal of the Royal Air Force	Lord Newall, who served with 2GR for nine years before transferring to the RAF
Diplomatic Corps	Sir Michael Scott (former Ambassador to Nepal and Malawi)
Lord Justice of Appeal	The Rt Hon Lord Templeman
Fellow of All Souls College, Oxford	Profesor R. Needham
Writing	John Masters
	John (C.J.) Morris
	Field-Marshall the Viscount Slim
	Professor Sir Ralph Turner
	J. M. Marks
	Adrian Hayter
	Brig. Michael Roberts

Politics	Sir John Nott
	Richard Holme
	Sir James Scott-Hopkins
Television and films	Tony Hart
	Anthony Steel
	Bill Travers
Explorer, soldier of fortune	Sir Hugh Boustead (one-time 4 GR)
Sport	P. J. Kininmonth (Captain of Scotland's Rugby after the Second World War)

And, if we include sons and daughters, there is the lovely Joanna Lumley, whose unstinting work for numerous charities has to be added to her well-deserved reputation as an actress and TV celebrity; Peter Winterbottom, current No. 7 in the England Rugby Union pack, and England cricketer Robin Jackman, the 'Surrey Sparrow', who was actually born in Simla. Their fathers all served with distinction in the Brigade. For others who may have been omitted in error, the author and the Regimental Association Secretaries ask forgiveness.

Although the concept of only having seconded officers for the Infantry regiments had been totally rejected in the early days of the Emergency, nevertheless Commanding Officers have learnt to appreciate that there is merit in having one or two officers from British units on secondment for sound reasons. For a start, fresh ideas are injected which can stop the battalion from becoming too parochial, while the seconded officer himself learns much that he can take away with him to his own parent unit, including a genuine feeling for the Gurkha soldiers. One or two seconded officers have returned to the Brigade in order to fill specific appointments at times when officers of the permanent cadre were not available in those particular age groups. An officer who had just completed a tour on secondment wrote:

Infantry officers will always volunteer for service with Gurkhas, for, like their predecessors, they know that they will serve with soldiers who still regard hard work, enthusiasm, loyalty, good manners and cheerfulness as sufficient motive for service. It is as simple as that.

Any officer who can suggest fresh ideas to challenge systems which have become a little rusty or introduce new methods is to be welcomed. Occasionally—and it is only occasionally—the seconded officers find one or two of the permanent cadre officers narrow-minded, regimentally dogmatic in outlook, the subject of bored smiles and tired grins in the offices of the sophisticated. However, were it not for the dedication and regimental pride of such officers, added to the backbone of solidness of the Gurkha himself, such an institution as the Brigade of Gurkhas could never have lasted so long. In the past there have been several British officers who served continuously with their regiments, or in appointments within the Brigade, disdaining promotion, scorning the over-inflated letters 'p.s.c.' (Passed Staff College), while maintaining the same high standards they had learnt as young officers in an ever-changing world. Those sahibs were good in action, they understood their men and led them with an affectionate but firm relationship that is hard to describe, all the time being influenced by the fact that they belonged to a regiment which, in their opinion, was second to none in the whole Army.

As we have seen, in the two World Wars Emergency Commissioned Officers came into the Brigade from all walks of life, some being experienced men in their own professions, others mere schoolboys. Inevitably a few failed to measure up to the exacting standards of the Brigade but when one considers the large numbers involved, the Gurkha soldiers were fortunate that the vast majority of their 'wartime sahibs' more than lived up to the best tradition of the regiments concerned.

Since the Second World War, the Brigade of Gurkhas has been represented on several Himalayan expeditions. With John Hunt's 1953 expedition, which conquered Everest for the first time, marched Charles Wylie of the 10th Gurkha Rifles and Jimmy Roberts of the 2nd Gurkhas; in 1970 a joint British and Royal Nepalese Army expedition tackled Annapurna under Bruce Niven, also from the 10th Gurkha Rifles; five years later, a party of British Army climbers grappled with Everest under the leadership of Tony Streather who previously had served a secondment with the 6th Gurkha Rifles. On this expedition the 7th Gurkhas were represented by one officer, Mike Kefford, and three Gurkha corporals, all of whom were included as climbers, while another nine Gurkha other ranks from other regiments and corps carried out a variety of duties in the 'support' group. In the end it was to be two SAS corporals who reached the summit, Bronco Lane and Brummie Stevens, but like all those who had achieved the feat before, they were quick to stress that the efforts of the whole party had been instrumental in getting them to the summit.

Far removed from the climbing fraternity was a most unusual sahib by the name of Henry Rokely Bond, who had been commissioned as a TA gunner officer way back in the mid-1920s. During the war he became a mountain gunner in the Indian Army and after seeing active service in Burma as a major, he drifted across to Malaya in 1948 and it was here that he met the 7th Gurkha Rifles for the first time, to begin an association which was to last until he died in 1979.

To the Regiment, and indeed to the Brigade as a whole, he was known as 'Bondo'. Bondo was a character out of a book, a bachelor of means who found retirement impossible and had come back voluntarily to serve without pay or pension, taking pride in being part of a Regiment once more while running and equipping the MT Platoon, often out of his own pocket. Some would say that authority treated him shoddily; besides no pension and no pay he had to sign an annual certificate to the effect that he would neither claim anything against the Army in the case of an accident nor would he be medically treated in the case of illness. Authority did relent in the late autumn of his life. His generosity was a byword and some would say that he was far too kind! A genial man, a sahib of the old school, Bondo's red face and white hair could be seen by all and sundry as he stood as No. 1 gunner in the scout cars that escorted the convoys through some of the most dangerous roads at the height of the Emergency in Malaya. He risked his life more than most and was always welcome in the out-company bases of the 1/7th Gurkha Rifles. Perhaps the bandits were deterred by the Popski-like figure who stood behind his home-made machine gun mounting in the leading vehicle; sufficient to say that the convoys worked like clockwork under his supervision. As far as the Gurkhas in the company bases were concerned it was '*Baje Sahib aunu bhayo*' (Grandfather Sahib has come), greeting him like a long-lost friend.

Bondo was to receive the MBE for years of faithful service running the MT Platoon and then the Officers' Mess; but since he was on no one's payroll, it had to be a civilian award. Perhaps the strangest thing about Bondo was that he never learnt to speak Nepali, but continued with his special brand of Hindustani in spite of years spent with his beloved Gurkhas. That notwithstanding, he was one of a very small band of officers to be remembered in the hills even after his death.

He was a character who had a deep knowledge of the Brigade and his Regiment, and had a fund of anecdotes about a vast number of officers and men who had served with him. On his death an officer was to write: 'Never had a Regiment as loyal a friend as Bondo.'

Although the easy relationship based on mutual respect between the British officer and his men is something that the Brigade takes for granted, it is not easy to explain to an outsider. In illustration of this, there have been several cases of young and apparently efficient officers who, after serving on a secondment or a short-service commission, have failed to gain approval—in particular of the Gurkha officers. More often than not this has been caused by the young man driving the men hard rather than leading them with a gentle but firm hand. However, sometimes such a failure to achieve rapport is caused by intangible reasons verging on snobbery.

The Colonel of a Regiment was asked by the CO of one of his battalions to discuss a certain young officer with the Gurkha Major because the latter firmly opposed the idea of the young man becoming a Permanent Cadre officer in the Regiment. The Colonel began the conversation:

'Why are you against Lieutenant Blank Sahib becoming a Permanent Cadre officer? To me he appears to have bags of enthusiasm and, I gather, is an extremely good games player.'

'Yes, Sahib. He is truly enthusiastic and, yes, he is in two of the Battalion teams as well as being a good runner.'

'I hear he is more than a good games player, that he will probably play for the Army at hockey in Hong Kong,' said the Colonel.

The Gurkha Major nodded before replying: 'A good games player, I agree.' Then he hesitated before continuing, 'He queries referees' decisions and behaves in a manner I don't expect to see from a British officer in our *paltan* [regiment]. Colonel Sahib, Lieutenant Blank may do well in a *gora paltan* (British battalion) but he is not for us.' An even longer pause ensued before he added most emphatically: 'Lieutenant Blank is not a Sahib!'

There was nothing more to be said. Lieutenant Blank did not join that Regiment as a Permanent Cadre officer!

The mixture of respect and informality, on whatever the occasion, continues even when the British and Gurkha officers are enjoying parties together. On a certain Guest Night, the Gurkha Officers were being entertained by their British counterparts and representatives from both messes were playing a game of 'Moriaty', the two contestants being blindfolded and lying near each other on the floor. A QGO, having been the recipient of a good hearty whack on his head from his opponent, politely asked: 'Are you there, Moriaty Sahib?' The mildness of the question did not stop him giving the young British officer an even heartier thump on the head.

An officer of a British regiment, who before the War had served alongside the 4th Gurkhas on the North-West Frontier, attended a party in the British Officers' Mess, after which he wrote:

> I believe the British officer who serves with Gurkhas to be one of the most remarkable—and certainly the most hardy—individuals that I have ever met ... This remarkable breed of men could celebrate—and still can, I have no doubt—until five and six in the morning: and then, with complete aplomb and certainty of purpose go on a Birthday Parade or lead a company in mock, or real, attack with absolute assurance of success. At one of their barbaric festivals they would sing and dance and imbibe all night with their beloved Gurkhas, in complete harmony and without ever jeopardising their positions as officers and men, and then lead them in every aspect of peace or war. . . . Great workers, great disciplinarians and great leaders—esteemed, loyally and steadfastly followed and completely trusted by their men—they were, as I have indicated, if the proper occasion and time arose, great revellers.

'The old and bold' will affirm that there are not so many parties now as there used to be in days gone by but such statements are the prerogative of the elderly and have been made since the beginning of time.

No one, especially an ex-officer of the Brigade, would be brave or foolhardy enough to select a few names of famous Gurkha officers who have served the Brigade over the years. The challenge would be an impossible one because each Regiment would have their own contenders and each Regiment would be right. That one particular Gurkha officer has been singled out for inclusion is not only because of his magnificent record of service but also because one of his sons was to become the first Gurkha Commissioned Officer to attend the Staff College at Camberley, which was to lead to him reaching his present rank of Lieutenant-Colonel in the British Army. With a father and son combination like that, perhaps the other Regiments in the Brigade will excuse Honorary Lt. Tikajit Pun being singled out for mention.

During 1943 Tikajit was one who emerged from the first Wingate expedition with honour, earning an IDSM (Indian Distinguished Service Medal) for gallantry before reaching the safety of India with the remnants of his unit. Rebuilding that Battalion after its traumatic experiences was a daunting task as inevitably a great deal of its spirit and confidence had been lost. Tikajit was one of the VCOs (GOs) chosen to help bring the unit back to its normal state of efficiency, a hectic period during which he did not spare himself, though never asking too much of the men under his command. It must be remembered, too, that there were difficulties in running a battalion with only two pre-war regular British officers so that it was from such Gurkha officers as Tikajit that the young wartime officers learnt so much. As a consequence, when the Battalion went back into Burma it won great renown during the battle of Snowdom when Bhanbhagta Gurung gained his VC. Tikajit Pun played a major but unobtrusive part in that battle honour won by the 3/2nd Gurkha Rifles. The CO at the time wrote:

I remember him steadfast, imperturbable under small arms fire and bombardment. I remember his championing of Riflemen in the Orderly Room ... I remember taking him with me to visit companies before attack and seeing how he could inspire Gurkhas to that cocky, nonchalant bravery which has brought success to many a desperate plan. But above all, I remember more clearly than anything else his compassion. I remember him with the wounded, tears behind his eyes, as he soothed those uncomplaining Gurkhas who, hiding their pain as always from the eyes of the onlooker, suffered in silence. . . . He was one of the greatest Gurkhas I have ever met and he served the Regiment to the uttermost of his exceptional ability.

Tikajit died in 1976; by that time his son had reached the rank of Lieutenant-Colonel, having already won the Military Cross during the Confrontation in Borneo. Tikajit took exceptional pride in his son's doings and both men will be remembered by their Regiment 'while memory serves'.

It is to the British Crown that the Gurkha swears allegiance, not to the Government in Whitehall, and it is an oath that is rarely broken.

The respect and affection shown for '*Hamro Maharani*' (Our Queen) is reflected in the number of pictures of Queen Elizabeth II that are displayed in so many ex-servicemen's homes in the hills of Nepal. Such loyalty was always so, as this story recalls. A Captain (QGO) of the 7th Gurkhas was visiting his wife at the civil hospital in Seremban (Malaya) on the day that King George VI died. Indeed, until that very morning, the Gurkha officer had been a KGO, as opposed to the present-day title reflecting the Queen on our throne. On emerging from the hospital at eleven o'clock, he remembered that there was to be a two-minute silence so, at the side of the road by himself, he stood to attention. Afterwards he remarked that the local Malays and Chinese had stared at him and passed remarks but that had not mattered; what had worried him most was that he had not been wearing a black armband and he felt that this omission detracted from his mark of respect to the late monarch, a King he had never seen but to whom he had given his oath of allegiance back in 1947, when he transferred from the Indian to the British Army.

Let us turn the clock forward to the present day. The Prince of Wales was visiting Pokhara towards the end of 1980 where, in his capacity as Colonel-in-Chief of the Second Gurkhas, he was meeting dozens of distinguished ex-soldiers who had come from far and wide to see him. There was a man, dressed almost biblically, standing in the queue to meet the Prince, who duly put out his hand, but the man did not respond. He was asked more than once what his old regiment was but initially he refused to answer. Then, scowling as he spoke, he said he belonged to no regiment because he had never been enlisted. The Prince, through an interpreter, then asked him why he was in the military camp.

'Come to meet you,' was the abrupt answer. After further question-ing it transpired that the man had walked four days to see the Prince—'We all knew you were coming'—and until that day he had never seen people shaking hands. An observer reported that the Prince of Wales was more impressed by that incident than most others that occurred during his short visit to Nepal.

Captain (GQO) Dipakbahadur Gurung of the Gurkha Transport Regiment, later to be a QGOO, in an article once posed the question: 'What makes the Gurkhas such fine soldiers and so loyal to a foreign country and people?' His answer was that

The British officers make the Gurkhas such fine soldiers. My father, who was a Captain (QGO) in the British Army in India, used to refer to the British officers as *Angrejbahadurs* (The brave Englishmen). People think that the Gurkhas are exceptionally brave soldiers but the Gurkhas in their hearts concede that the British officers are equally brave.

Dipakbahadur goes on to elaborate, describing the qualities that he expects to find in his British officers, before ending on this note:

He is a real master and friend who never betrays his men whatever the odds are. The maintenance of this image by the British officers has been more or less responsible for the survival of the Brigade so far. To maintain such an image is a challenge to the British officers today.

No one who has studied the Brigade's history would disagree with what Dipakbahadur has written. Quite rightly he emphasizes how important it is to select the right British officers, adding that, 'The standard of the Brigade and the Gurkhas depends much more on the quality of the British officers'. In return, nearly every British officer would claim that the standard of the Gurkha officers can make or break a unit.

And so we return to the man, for the vast majority of those who enlist in the British Army do not become Gurkha officers, because the vacancies are comparatively few and as they are all long-term regulars, room at the top is limited. The majority of the Gurkhas serving in the 1980s have changed very little; they rarely settle in foreign lands nor do more than a handful even marry foreign nationals. After retiring from the Army, they return to Nepal. But some of the younger men recently enlisted, being far better educated and with little or no knowledge of the tough life endured by their parents and ancestors, undoubtedly view the conservative ideas of the Brigade as being an anachronism. One senior officer has said that it is by no means a problem yet but it is something that will need to be watched. That small handful apart, the present-day Gurkha soldiers, being better educated, admirably fit into the needs of the modern British Army and certainly are not resting on the reputation of their fore-fathers.

Together with his respect for his superiors is the average Gurkha's belief in fate, although this may only come to the surface when he is sick or in dire misfortune. Captain Maniprasad Rai commented:

> Then one hears words like: '*Mero dasa lageko thiyo, Sahib*' (I was fated with this calamity) or '*Yatinai samma pugna bhanera lekheko rahechha*' (Fate must have written down that I was to reach only so far and no more). In ordinary circumstances, such fatalism can be of great assistance to him as a soldier when things are going badly, but, as has been mentioned before, there are times, especially in sickness or after being badly wounded, when he decides that the end has come—it's no use fighting fate— whereas a European might take a much more positive stand against the slings and arrows of misfortune.

If the Gurkhas are as loyal, faithful, hard-working and ready to go into battle as ever before, then it would be right to attribute a large share of their prowess in battle to absolute obedience to orders and loyalty to their leaders. Being an officer in the Brigade of Gurkhas is highly rewarding, but it is a challenge and undoubtedly the Gurkhas expect their officers to be of the highest calibre. For such a reason did Dipakbahadur state that it is the British officers who make the Gurkhas such fine soldiers. Perhaps it is better to say that they form an ideal partnership and have done so since 1815. Long may it continue.

It has become almost traditional to end any book or article about the Gurkhas by quoting the much-loved words written by Professor Sir Ralph Turner MC, who was adjutant in the 2/3rd QAO GR during the First World War. However, two poems were received during the compilation of this book, both written by old soldiers, one British and the other Gurkha. Bill Winchester saw active service with the 10th Indian Division in Italy during 1943 and calls his 'Salute to a Gurkha'. Bishan Dewan, who served with the 10th Gurkhas, entitles his 'A Tribute to a Hillman'. Their poems are too long to reproduce but both have been written in a spirit of love and respect.

Bill Winchester's poem tells us how a stocky little man from the mountains of Nepal dies on the field of battle. He ends in this way:

> On his grave they placed his kukri,
> Seemed the right kind of thing to do,
> If he had known the way we felt,

> He would have been proud too.
>
> ...
>
> And pray the sacrifice he made,
> Was not blood vainly shed
> And may the Gurkhas be remembered
> With England's own brave dead!

The poem written by Bishan Dewan follows a hillman not to war but back to his village. Although understandably Bisham finds the writing of poetry in a foreign tongue none too easy, the sincerity is there. For those of us who live in the affluent surroundings of the United Kingdom, surely these words have a message:

> Social Security, old-age pension and National Health
> Are only for people who have the wealth.
> Storms and snow, floods and a slide,
> Insurance is a word that hasn't arrived.

And so to Sir Ralph Turner's preface to the Nepali dictionary he began to compile while serving with his battalion in the Middle East.

> My thoughts return to you who were my comrades, the stubborn and indomitable peasants of Nepal. ... Once more I hear the laughter with which you greeted every hardship. Once more I see you in your bivouacs or about your fires, on forced march or in the trenches, now shivering with wet and cold, now scorched by a pitiless and burning sun. Uncomplaining you endure hunger and thirst and wounds; and at the last your unwavering lines disappear into the smoke and wrath of battle. Bravest of the brave, most generous of the generous, never had a country more faithful friends than you.

ELEVEN

Epilogue: The Brigade Today and Tomorrow

It is far easier to report on the Brigade of today (early 1984) than it is to peer into the uncertain future. 'What we look for does not come to pass. God finds a way for what none foresaw,' wrote Euripides over 400 years before Christ and his message is as true today as it was then. We are in the present. We cannot tell what the morrow will bring forth, and it is probably better that way.

At the time of writing, the bulk of the Brigade is stationed in Hong Kong and its adjoining New Territories so that their future is inextricably linked with that of the Colony. There, three infantry battalions provide security and stability in support of the police as well as keeping in touch with the outer world by sending sub-units on military exercises annually to Fiji, Australia, New Zealand, Brunei and Papua–New Guinea. Assistance to the civil community is given a high priority. All units participate in such projects although, for obvious reasons, the major construction works are carried out by the Queen's Gurkha Engineers, utilizing their sophisticated plant and highly developed technical skills.

Over the South China Sea in Brunei there is another battalion living in accommodation built and paid for by the Sultan's Government, which also meets most other expenses. The training facilities in Brunei are excellent, so that jungle warfare techniques are kept alive, especially in the Temburong district which over the years has witnessed several stirring exercises, involving movement on land, sea, air and along the waterways of the hinterland. The tour in Brunei provides a welcome change from the confined urban spaces of Hong Kong where training areas fast disappear so that even the most imaginative of commanders finds it increasingly difficult to avoid repetition and its handmaiden, boredom.

As already described, the fifth battalion serves a two-year tour in the UK and some of their exploits have been covered in Chapter 7. The UK-based battalion has played an important part in the UK Land Forces order of battle (for example, the Falklands, Belize and a battalion exercise in BAOR, planned for late 1984). In addition, the Brigade provides two Demonstration Companies at Sandhurst and Brecon where most of the men serve a year's tour, doing work which is often exacting and invariably in the public eye.

To speculate about the future would be dangerous and pointless. In a previous book, *Britain's Brigade of Gurkhas*, I was optimistic enough to affirm, 'It looks certain that the Brigade will continue to serve the British Crown for some years to come', and those words were written in 1971 when the outlook was just as uncertain as the present day.

Today, some fourteen years later, no one can deny that the horizon is shrouded in doubt but this is something that the officers and men of the Brigade have learned to live with ever since they became part of the British Army back in 1948. At that time there were several sages who stated that the uncertain political situation in India and Nepal would mean that the newly-raised British Brigade was unlikely to be in existence for more than five years at the most. Thirty-five years later similar comments are still made. The most important fact to report is that the officers and men serving today are not diverted by unfounded rumours or cast down by idle speculation, knowing well that their task is to uphold the professional standards which have been established over the years, wherever Gurkhas have served the British Crown.

One day fate will decide to end this long, happy and unique partnership but until it does the standard of the Gurkha soldiers will continue to be second to none. Witness this report, written by an NCO about one of his students on a potential NCO's Cadre in Hong Kong.

He was as light as a butterfly, as quick as a rabbit, as cautious as a virgin and without doubt, came top among my squad. A soldier with such potential qualities should be a great asset to the Brigade!

Of one thing I am certain then, with men like that it is wise to be on the same side as the Gurkhas.

APPENDIX A

Origin of the Gurkha Regiments and Corps

The Gurkha Regiments and Corps in the British Army

Throughout the nineteenth century there were many intricate changes in titles. To have shown all those details would require a long and elaborate appendix, and one that might be a little too involved for the average reader.

2nd King Edward IV Own Gurkha Rifles (the Sirmoor Rifles)
Raised at Nahan, Sirmoor, in early 1815 by Lieutenant Frederick Young from hillmen, mainly Kumaonis and Garhwalis who had fought under the Nepalese General Amarsing Thapa against Sir David Ochterlony. These men, having been captured by the British during the war with Nepal, were held in camps in Sirmoor and Dehra Dun. Thereafter the Regiment's 'home' was at Dehra Dun at the foot of the Himalayas until 1947.

6th Queen Elizabeth's Own Gurkha Rifles
This was one of the old Assam regiments whose title changed many times. Raised by Captain Fraser at Chaubiajganj in Cuttack, Orissa, in 1817 as the Cuttack Legion. In 1828 it became the Assam Local Light Infantry and in 1886, the 42nd Gurkha Light Infantry. Its 'home' was later to be at Abbottabad until joining the British Army in 1947.

7th Duke of Edinburgh's Own Gurkha Rifles
One of the Burma battalions, raised in 1902 at Thayetmyo in Burma by Major E. Vansittart as the 8th Gurkha Rifles. Its 'home' was

eventually in Quetta, Baluchistan, followed by moves dictated by the Second World War that ended in 1947 when the Regiment left India for the last time.

10th Princess Mary's Own Gurkha Rifles

One of the Burma battalions. Raised in 1890 by Lieutenant-Colonel C. R. Macgregor as the 1st Burma Infantry. In 1901 became the 10th Gurkha Rifles. Its 'home' was at first at Maymyo in Burma, later at Quetta, before moving to the Kangra Valley as its last centre in India, prior to 1947.

The Queen's Gurkha Engineers

Gurkhas were first enlisted into the Royal Engineers in 1948 when 67 Field Squadron RE was formed at Kluang (Malaya) during October of that year. The first squadron was formed from Gurkha infantrymen who were attached to the Royal Engineers and wore the RE cap badge.

The Queen's Gurkha Signals

Raised in November, 1948, when a small cadre of one Royal Signals officer and eight soldiers, together with seven Gurkha soldiers from infantry battalions, provided the training team which led to the Gurkha Signals of today.

The Gurkha Transport Regiment

The Gurkha Transport Regiment, formerly The Gurkha Army Service Corps, was formed as a component part of the Brigade of Gurkhas in July, 1958, with volunteers from Gurkha infantry battalions under RASC officers, seconded to the Gurkha Army Service Corps.

General

The 2nd and 6th Gurkha Rifles enlist the majority of their men from the Magar and Gurung clans of Western Nepal, while the 7th and 10th Gurkhas attract most of their recruits from among the Kiranti tribes of East Nepal, the majority of whom are Limbus and Rais. The three Corps are composed of an approximately equal mixture from East and West Nepal.

The Indian Army Gurkha Brigade

1st King George IV Own Gurkha Rifles (the Malaun Regiment)
Raised at Sabbathu, near Simla, by Lieutenant R. Ross in early 1815 from hillmen, mainly Kumaonis and Garhwalis. The home cantonment of this Regiment was later sited at Dharmsala in the Kangra Valley. This regiment's title changed many times during the nineteenth century.

3rd Queen Alexandra's Own Gurkha Rifles
Raised at Almora, Kumaon, in early 1815 by Lieutenant Sir R. Colquhoun, Bt, from hillmen who took service with the British after the conquest of Kumaon by Colonel Jasper Nichols during the Nepal War. In General Tuker's opinion, this Regiment could be the oldest of the Gurkha Brigade by a month or two; he claims that its 'birth' took place in late 1814 when Colonel Gardener was attacking Almora. Officially, however, it was raised by Colquhoun a few days after the 1st and 2nd Gurkha Rifles. Inevitably, its 'home' was at Almora.

The 4th Prince of Wales' Own Gurkha Rifles
Raised at Pithorgarah, Kumaon, ten miles from the Nepal border, in 1857 by Lieutenant D. Macintyre as the Extra Gurkha Regiment, renamed the 4th Gurkha Regiment shortly afterwards. Its 'home' was at Bakloh, close to the hill station of Dalhousie.

5th Royal Gurkha Rifles
Raised in 1857 at Abbottabad in the North-West Frontier Province, by Captain H. W. F. Boisragon as the Hazara Gurkha Battalion. This Regiment was the only one of the pre-1947 Indian Brigade to belong to the old Punjab Frontier Force. Its 'home' was at Abbottabad, and it became 'Royal' in 1923.

8th Gurkha Rifles
Another of the old Assam regiments. Raised at Sylhet in Assam in 1824 by Captain P. Dudgeon as the Sylhet Local Battalion. In 1886 it became the 44th Gurkha Light Infantry. The Second Battalion was raised in 1835 and later became the 43rd Gurkha Light Infantry. General Tuker remarks that it was the oldest of the Second Battalions in the British-Indian Gurkha Brigade. Its 'home' was at Shillong in Assam.

9th Gurkha Rifles

One of the old Bengal battalions. Raised at Fatehgarh in the United Provinces in 1817 by Major C. S. Fagan as the Fatehgarh Levy. It became the 9th Gurkha Rifles in 1901 and its 'home' was later established at Dehra Dun. The only regiment to recruit the higher-cast Chhetris and Thakurs.

11th Gurkha Rifles

This Regiment was formed for a short time in the First World War and later re-formed from those men in the 7th and 10th Gurkha Rifles who, in 1947, opted to remain in the post-Independent Indian Army. The bulk of their men were from East Nepal.

Apart from the 11th Gurkha Rifles, the other Regiments of the Indian Army continue to enlist the majority of their men from Western Nepal, although exact details of the breakdown are not known.

APPENDIX B

The Gurkha Welfare Scheme

(These notes are reproduced from a paper prepared by HQ Brigade of Gurkhas with their kind permission.)

General

The Gurkha Welfare Scheme is an organization established by the Brigade of Gurkhas to ensure the rapid and responsible investigation of reports of distress and hardship among Gurkha ex-servicemen and their dependants, and to disburse such funds as are considered necessary to relieve such hardship and distress. Within Nepal the scheme is controlled by the Commander British Gurkhas Nepal on behalf of the Major-General Brigade of Gurkhas.

There are twenty-three Welfare Centres in Nepal and two in India. Centres are staffed by an Area Welfare Officer (AWO), Welfare Assistant, Medical Assistant, Welfare Centre Orderly, and in some Centres there is an Agricultural Assistant.

Finances

The Welfare Scheme receives *no* money from the British Government or Ministry of Defence (MOD) for payment of welfare grants or pensions. Only a small annual grant for the payment of welfare staff salaries and for the maintenace of Welfare Centres is received.

Gurkha Welfare Trusts. The Brigade of Gurkhas launched a series of appeals in 1967 with the objects of raising £1,000,000. Before launching this appeal the Brigade raised approx £300,000 from its own resources. The capital of the Gurkha Welfare Trusts is now over £3m. This money is now invested in the UK and other countries, is administered by the Gurkha Welfare Trustees and provides the main source of income for the GWS (currently £155,000) per year.

One Day's Pay Scheme. Every serving soldier in the Brigade of Gurkhas from the MGBG to the latest-joined recruit gives one day's pay per year to the GWT: currently £28,000.

MOD Grant. The MOD (Army) gives an annual grant to cover the pay and allowances of welfare staff, and the rent and maintenance of welfare staff, and the rent and maintenance of Welfare Centres; any balance may be spent on welfare medicines. *None* of this money can be used for individual welfare grants or pensions.

The Gurkha Welfare Trust Foundation (USA). The Gurkha Welfare Trust Foundation (USA) was established through the generosity of Mr and Mrs Ellice Macdonald Jnr. They both take a very active and personal interest in Gurkha welfare and attend the annual Gurkha Welfare Trustees meeting in London. The Trustees of the Foundation welcome requests from the Commander British Gurkhas Nepal to fund special projects and are now funding the cost of medicines (£10,500 p.a.) provided at Welfare Centres.

Gurkka Welfare Trust (Canada). The Gurkha Welfare Trust (Canada) annual budget controlled by HQ BRIGNEPAL amounts to nearly £115,000.

The Kadoorie Foundation. The Kadoorie Foundation was established in Hong Kong by the Kadoorie family. Mr Horace Kadoorie, brother of Lord Kadoorie, is Chairman or Director of numerous Hong Kong companies ranging from Hong Kong & Shanghai Hotels Ltd to Hutchison Whampoa Limited. He came into contact with the Brigade through his offer to provide training in agriculture and animal husbandry in Hong Kong to Gurkha soldiers prior to their return to Nepal on discharge. He visits Nepal each year and now donates up to £160,000 annually to various welfare projects in Nepal (see also p. 173).

Student Grants. A total of about £16,000 is paid out annually for student grants from eight different Student Grant Funds.

How the scheme works

The Welfare Scheme is *not* an insurance policy to compensate for losses. It is basically a 'first aid' scheme to help an ex-serviceman or his dependants survive a personal loss or tragedy. A welfare pension can be awarded to an ex-serviceman or his dependants who through sickness, injury or age are unable to support themselves and have no one else to support them. No one has an automatic right to welfare aid; every case is dealt with on its merits and help can only be given after a thorough investigation into the case and the financial circumstances of the individual concerned. A rich man can expect little or no aid if he suffers a loss but still has considerable land or property remaining. The poor man who has lost all can expect the maximum aid possible. Help can not be given in every case due to limited funds—but every case is investigated thoroughly and treated on its merits.

Eligible persons
All ex-servicemen of the Brigade of Gurkhas, Gurkha Contingent Singapore Police, and certain civilian employees are eligible for welfare aid within the current rules. Gurkha ex-servicemen who served in any of the ten regiments of the old Indian Army Gurkha Brigade, Assam Rifles, Assam Regiment, Burma Rifles and Burma Frontier Force prior to 15 August, 1947, are also eligible for aid. Dependants of these groups may also receive aid. Dependants are parents who are unable to fend for themselves due to illness or age, a legal wife or widow, who has not subsequently re-married, and children. Although a person may be eligible, he or she will not automatically receive the aid—this must always depend on a thorough investigation and the applicant's financial circumstances.

Type of situation where aid may be given
Assistance may be given in the following circumstances: death of breadwinner—only aid will be given for funeral expenses or death ceremonies but a grant or welfare pension may be given if the family is destitute; house destroyed by fire; land damaged by flood or landslide; certain very expensive medical treatment, but only with prior sanction of Deputy Recruiting Officers (DROs); famine; accident, injury or sickness which results in the individual concerned being unable to support himself or his family.

Aid will *not* normally be given for: hail damage or crop failure, unless this results in famine or the family concerned are completely destitute.

Welfare medicines
Welfare medicines are purchased from funds supplied by GWT

Foundation USA, MOD (A) grant and GWT (UK). Welfare medicines are given to all ex-servicemen of the Brigade of Gurkhas, Singapore Police and certain former locally employed civilians, i.e., schoolteachers, midwives, etc., and their dependants. Singapore Police and the civilians listed are eligible, as they contribute to the ODPS. Welfare Centres are supplied on a quarterly basis and when supplies run out they cannot be replaced until the next quarter. Serving soldiers are not entitled to receive any aid from GWT funds; nor (except in emergencies) are they allowed to receive welfare medicines.

Kadoorie Foundation

The Kadoorie Foundation has grown up as a personal extension of Mr Horace Kadoorie's appreciation of the stabilizing role played by Gurkha troops in Hong Kong during the past 15 years. Mr Kadoorie, on his annual visit to Nepal, usually agrees to finance a number of individual and community-orientated projects recommended by the Commander British Gurkhas Nepal. He also gives large sums to finance projects and individuals recommended by the managers of the ODM's farms at Lumle in West Nepal and Pakhribas in East Nepal.

Conclusion

By dint of the generosity of countless friends and supporters all over the world, the Gurkha Welfare Scheme has an annual income of about £450,000 (1983). Long may such ready support be forthcoming.

APPENDIX C

The Kukri

(This article is reproduced with the kind permission of HQ Brigade of Gurkhas from their information booklet *The Brigade of Gurkhas*.)

In 1767–8 Prithwi Narayan Shah, King of the Gurkhas, invaded the Nepal Valley and, although encountering superior forces, he succeeded in conquering his enemies and, one by one, the towns of the valley fell to his superior fighting ability, culminating in the fall of Kathmandu in 1768. Prithwi Narayan thus became the first King of Nepal who combined the country of the Gurkhas and the Nepal Valley and much of the kingdom as it exists today.

When Prithwi Narayan invaded the valley, he encountered soldiers armed with the traditional edged weapons of that period, heavy two-edged swords, long spears, wrist-guard daggers and short, straight single-edged swords. Prithwi Narayan's soldiers carried a compara-tively new weapon, a short oddly-curved knife, and the inability of his enemies to develop a parry for this knife, known as the kukri, was, in some measure at least, responsible for their defeat. As long as edged weapons continued as the principal arm of soldiers, the kukri remained superior in hand-to-hand conflict.

Its efficiency as a fighting weapon caused it to be adopted as the national weapon of Nepal and even now every soldier in the army of Nepal and Britain's Brigade of Gurkhas is issued with a serviceable kukri of good steel. Today most 'hill' people and valley dwellers still carry a kukri in their belts or sashes and use it for all purposes—butchering, defence against wild animals, tree cutting and the peeling of vegetables—in fact, an all-purpose instrument. When the King of Nepal is absent from any official festival or ceremony a gold *kukri* (the King's own) is reverently placed on his throne and obeisance is made thereto by his family and ministers; officially the King, through his *kukri*, is present.

The earliest known kukri, preserved in the National Museum in Kathmandu, belonged to Rajadradas Shah, King of Gorkha in 1627. It is a heavy, broad-bladed kukri with a carved wooden handle and has the traditional peculiar curve and notched guard at the base of the blade.

The shape of the kukri has changed but little since 1627; the notch near the handle and the groove along the edge of the blade are invariably present. The size and weight vary depending upon its destined use and the handles vary in material—wood, bone, ivory and rhino horn being used with a variety of carving and inlay of semi-precious stone. The scabbard is found in leather, wood and bone, always the same shape but variably tooled, carved and adorned. Some are very ornately embellished with gold or brass filigree work and heavily set with turquoise, coral, lapis lazuli and coloured glass. When the handle is carved it usually represents an animal's head with mother-of-pearl eyes, the mouth open, teeth bared and tongue protruding.

The standard scabbard contains a pocket partitioned to receive a leather purse and two small knives; one dull-edged for a hone and the other sharp for small cutting jobs. Sometimes a third pocket contains a pair of tweezers.

The notch near the base of the blade is responsible for much of the kukri's efficiency; the blow of an opponent's sword, sabre or dagger is caught on the kukri blade and slipped down into the notch when a quick twist will disarm the opponent.

The kukris of Royalty and high officers of the Nepalese Army can usually be distinguished by exquisite etching and engraving on the blade and frequently the circular insignia of the ruling caste or the half circles denoting army issue are found. The scabbards are gold and silver mounted and the handles frequently are inlaid with two or more precious gems, usually emeralds. Another notable kukri which hangs in the Kathmandu museum belonged to Kaji Kalu Pande, a warrior active in 1749; it is exceptionally heavy with a very wide blade, razor sharp even today and stamps Pande as being quite a lusty gentleman to have been able to wield it.

The steel used for the kukri blades varies from a rather poor, locally-made steel which requires frequent honing to maintain its edge, to the finest of Continental steels.

There have been many myths about the kukri and the advertisement below (taken from an American magazine) is but one example.

World famous Gurkha fighting knife plus two skinning knives in one triple divided hand-tooled belt sheath—total weight: 2 lbs. Used, guar, excellent. It took one year to collect our small shipment of these deadly finely-balanced weapons from tribal villages in Khyber Pass region, 3 hand-forged curved and polished blades, 3 hand-carved white deer horn grips. Traditional Gurkha weapon used for centuries against Afghans, Persians other Indian races and in N. Africa against WW II German troops who dreaded the night-fighting Gurkhas. Length of main knife: 1½ ft. Excellent for hunting, camping, a never-again item for collectors.

Even at the height of Nepal's expansion at the end of the eighteenth century, her warriors did not reach the Khyber Pass.

Bestselling War Fiction and Non-Fiction

☐ Passage to Mutiny	Alexander Kent	£2.50
☐ The Flag Captain	Alexander Kent	£2.50
☐ Badge of Glory	Douglas Reeman	£2.50
☐ Winged Escort	Douglas Reeman	£2.50
☐ Army of Shadows	John Harris	£2.50
☐ Up for Grabs	John Harris	£2.50
☐ Decoy	Dudley Pope	£1.95
☐ Curse of the Death's Head	Rupert Butler	£2.25
☐ Gestapo	Rupert Butler	£2.75
☐ Auschwitz and the Allies	Martin Gilbert	£4.95
☐ Tumult in the Clouds	James A. Goodson	£2.95
☐ Sigh for a Merlin	Alex Henshaw	£2.50
☐ Morning Glory	Stephen Howarth	£4.95
☐ The Doodlebugs	Norman Longmate	£4.95
☐ Colditz – The Full Story	Major P. Reid	£2.95